MAMMALS

OF THE

SOUTHWEST DESERTS

TEXT

ILLUSTRATIONS BY DALE THOMPSON

Copyright 1982 by Southwest Parks and Monuments Association
ISBN 911408-60-6
Library of Congress Number 81-86094
Editorial: Rose Houk, T.J. Priehs, Carolyn Dodson
Design: McQuiston and Daughter, Inc.
Production: T.J Priehs, Don McQuiston, Debra McQuiston.
Lithography: Lorraine Press
Revised Edition: 1988

CONTENTS

INTRODUCTION

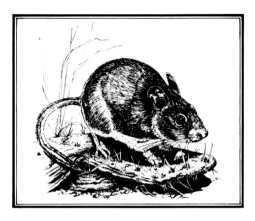

Wesst of the one-hundredth meridian, a line extending roughly through San Antonio and Oklahoma City, lies what cartographers of the nineteenth century called the "Great American Desert." The one unifying characteristic of this area of the southwestern United States and northern Mexico is its dryness. Given what author Joseph Wood Krutch called this "grand fact of dryness," it becomes more difficult to generalize about this region.

The primary element that creates desert conditions is scanty rainfall. In the Southwest two factors are mainly responsible: the high mountain barriers and the prevailing westerly winds. Moisture-laden air sweeping in from the Pacific Ocean is wrung dry as it rises over the high coastal ranges; only a few of the winter storms can surmount this barrier and carry rain to the desert. When these rains do arrive, they are usually gentle and may last a day or more.

The desert's violent summer storms, that produce flash floods, arise in the tropics, moving in from the south. They usually occur in July and August after a hot, parching period. Much of this moisture falls in the mountains. That which falls on the desert is often torrential but brief. Little precipitation from these storms soaks in to the baked earth. Most of it runs off and is channeled into rivers.

Though difficult to estimate, precipitation averages from less than 8 inches (20 centimeters) a year for the Lower Sonoran Zone to 15 inches (37.5 centimeters) annually in the Upper Sonoran. Areas in California's Mojave desert have gone without measurable rainfall for more than a year.

Low relative humidities—15 percent is not uncommon—result from this sparse rainfall and absence of bodies of water. Clouds rarely form, except during the rainy seasons. The few that may build up around the mountaintops are soon dissipated as they drift over the hot valleys.

Summer temperatures are high. In the Lower Sonoran Zone the thermometer often rises to 110°F (43.3°C). Ground surface temperatures soar to 150°F (65.6°C). With little haze for insulation or moisture to hold in the heat, temperatures drop quickly after the sun goes down. Day and nighttime temperatures commonly differ by as much as 20 to 30 degrees in the summer and even more in winter. The winters are mild, with freezing temperatures rare and cold spells short-lived.

Early naturalists divided North America into life zones, areas where elevational change marked distinctly different environments. While this concept has been changed and refined over the years, the initial categories are still useful for description. As used in this book, the lower Sonoran Zone is the region at sea level or below (Death Valley) to approximately 4500 feet. Cacti, trees like mesquite and palo verde, and drought-resistant shrubs are characteristic vegetation of the Lower Sonoran. Upper Sonoran Zone refers to the continuous border along the edges of the lower desert, extending from 4500 to 6500 feet (1373 to 1983 meters) in elevation. It consists mainly of four types of terrain: wide, gently sloping valleys, level mesas, low desert mountains and steep slopes circling the higher "island" mountains.

Although not literally part of the desert, another zone provides important habitat to animals. The Transition Zone lies between the Sonoran zones and the Canadian zones at altitudes of 6500 to 9000 feet (1983 to 2743 meters). Ponderosa pine, interspersed with oak and aspen, is the predominant vegetation. This zone is extensive in plateau country and at the higher elevations of the Basin and Range country. The Transition Zone is marked by annual precipitation of about 21 inches (53 centimeters), some of it snowfall, and mean temperatures of 60° F. (16° C).

Travelers through this North American desert may attribute uncomplimentary names to it and want to pass it by as quickly as possible. But a short sojourn in its environs reaps rewards, not the least of which is a beginning appreciation of its diversity.

Plants and desert-dwelling animals, living in this region of little rain and high temperatures, have evolved physical and behavioral traits that are quite different from similar species found in moister climates. To understand these differences it is necessary to know something of the land in which they live.

This book's geographic scope includes western Texas to the coastal range of California, from central Utah and Colorado to northern Mexico. Within this general area are five distinct deserts, three of which lie contiguous to the U.S. southern border and are actually extrusions of the great deserts of northern Mexico. The other two lie entirely within the United States and differ considerably in climate and in the plant species found in them. The three southern deserts include the *Chihuahuan,* the northern end of the Mexican desert of the same name. It extends north into New Mexico and west Texas, bounded on the east by the level lands of Texas and on the west by the Continental Divide. Among its wealth of cacti and succulent plants, *Agave lechuguilla* is considered an indicator plant.

The *Sonoran* desert, containing fine stands of saguaro cactus, the largest cactus native to the United States, covers much of the southern half of Arizona. The Continental Divide on the east and the Colorado River on the west can be considered its natural boundaries.

Actually an extension of the Sonoran desert, the *Colorado* desert lies in southern California, stretching from the Colorado River west to the coastal range and south into Baja California. The northern boundaries of this low, alkaline, saltbush-covered land run from the Little San Bernardino Mountains east to the Colorado River.

The two northern deserts are less sharply defined: the *Mojave* occupies much of southern Nevada and California from north of Death Valley south to the Little San Bernardino Mountains. In much of its low-lying basin, only the most drought-resistant plants can live. It contains the great sink known as Death Valley, one of the hottest and driest places on earth. Yearly rainfall averages only about 3 inches (7.5 centimeters).

The *Great Basin* desert, covering a large part of northern Nevada and extreme western Utah, is often referred to as a "cold" desert because of its higher elevations, covered with almost continuous sagebrush.

The adaptations animals have made to survive in the desert are especially interesting. While living with a diversity of vegetation, they must live with its austerity also. As a rule, mammals will remain in the vicinity where food is plentiful, except for carnivores which range more widely. Exceptions to this rule exist, of course, and are often found in the Southwest due to the highly specialized habits of a few of the desert species.

Kangaroo rats, for instance, live within a comparatively small area. The kit fox, which preys on them, will remain where the kangaroo rats are plentiful. Other medium-sized predators such as raccoons, coatis and coyotes are less restricted. Their omnivorous food habits, larger size and lack of dependence on a permanent home allow them this greater mobility. Larger predators, such as mountain lions and jaguars, stay in one locality only long enough to rear young. They often range hundreds of miles in search of new hunting grounds.

Other specialized creatures like the armadillo and hognosed skunk are found only where they are able to locate the insects and worms which make up the bulk of their diet. Other mammals may be associated with certain plants native to small, specific areas. Some of the species are not strictly indigenous to the desert but may be found over a wide range. However the desert forms will usually be paler in color and smaller.

This book is designed to help the amateur desert naturalist identify desert mammals. While not intended to be a scientific key, its illustrations and descriptions will aid in determining genus, if not species, of the animals included.

Common and scientific names are included for each animal. Latin names are a universal language to serious students of natural history. All mammal names consist of two or three parts. The first is the genus, or group to which the animal belongs; the second is the specific name, which identifies one member of the group; the third, if present, is the subspecific name or the variety of the species. Few subspecific forms have been described here unless a variety is so distinct from the type that it can easily be identified.

Only one or two of the most outstanding species of each group have been included in this book. More detailed information can be gained by consulting the references. The 42 mammals in this book represent 21 families and 8 orders. With apologies to mammalogists, some liberties have been taken in arrangement of the species.

WILDLIFE OBSERVATION

Visitors to the Southwest may at first be surprised to see so few animals during the day. Most are nocturnal, saving their activities until temperatures have dropped. An hour's quiet vigil, with a flashlight, can prove rewarding at night. Do not expect to see many mammals on windy nights, because the noise of the wind and rustling branches hides the sound of predators, causing most to stay under cover. The greatest animal activity is found just after the first summer rains.

National parks and monuments, where animals are protected in their natural surroundings, are excellent places to view wildlife. More information about animals that live in a specific park or monument can be obtained from park rangers and naturalists.

While observing animals, remember that their presence is for the enjoyment of everyone. Observe National Park Service rules which prohibit feeding of wildlife. The sweet, starchy food that well-meaning visitors usually offer can be harmful to animals. The wildlife are much better at finding food for themselves in their natural environment. Do not tease, harass or in any way disturb animals. Observe them, photograph them, and protect their habitats.

It is our hope that this guidebook will enhance your experience in the southwestern deserts and that it will encourage efforts to preserve the desert for its inhabitants. Former predator control programs, overhunting, overgrazing, and other encroachments of civilization have resulted in the decline in numbers of many wildlife species. As species extinctions increase, the values of native wildlife and its preservation become more apparent.

Peccary
Dicotyles tajacu

DESCRIPTION: A dark, piglike animal resembling a razorback hog, but with heavier neck and shoulders. Total length about 30 inches (75 centimeters), tail unnoticeable from a distance. Black and gray bristles blend to form a "salt-and-pepper" color, shading to black on lower legs. A lighter band of hair around the neck gives it the common name "collared peccary." A mane of long black hair on the back of the neck and shoulders bristles when the animal is alarmed or angry. Snout and eyes piglike. Both sexes, particularly old boars, develop tusks and have a large musk gland on the back near the rump. Weight about 50 pounds (22.5 kilograms) for an average mature male. Young, usually two, born primarily in July and August. Reddish brown when small, they gradually turn gray.

The smallest hooved mammals native to the Southwest, the peccaries have unique feet—they have four toes on the front foot and only three on the hind foot.

The heavy head and neck, also unique to peccaries, prevents them from rooting deeply without dropping to their knees. The hair is often worn off in these spots and old individuals often form a callus pad on the front legs.

A species thought to have migrated north from humid Mexican jungles, peccaries have to some degree adapted to the arid land they inhabit in the Southwest. Recent research indicates sufficient moisture may be obtained from succulent food for several days at a time. But access to free water is also necessary.

The two factors that determine what habitat they will occupy are food and shelter. Shrubs, grass, mesquite beans, cacti and various roots and tubers make up the peccaries' diet. They seem to be able to eat cactus, spines and all, without ill effects. Nuts and berries are also consumed in great quantities. In higher elevations, oaks supply acorns for several months.

Shelter, while not as important as food, is nevertheless a large factor in determining a javelina herd's location. The twisting courses of desert washes with their trees offer concealment to them. When the steep banks erode, cavities that are warm in winter and cool in summer are provided. Likewise, abandoned mine tunnels may be used, especially in summer.

Peccaries have poor eyesight but a keen sense of smell. When feeding, they scatter across an area in loose groups, the young staying close by their mothers. At the first scent of danger, they remain still and emit musk odors from the gland on the back and click their tusks. If cornered, they may charge the object or, more often, flee in all directions. Tales of peccary "attacks" are more likely the animals' confused efforts to escape danger.

RANGE: Southwestern Arizona and New Mexico; Texas.

HABITAT: Arid regions, isolated foothills.

Opossum
Didelphis virginiana

DESCRIPTION: About the size of a house cat, with a long, pointed nose and naked tail. Total length about 30 inches (75 centimeters); tail about 15 inches (37.5 centimeters). Generally a soft, dark gray to black color; lighter about the face. The black ears are rounded and thin. Eyes prominent and black. Feet are black, armed with sharp claws. Tail naked, flexible and prehensile.

The opossum is the only marsupial native to the United States. Under the female's belly is a pouch that encloses a single mammary gland with 13 nipples. After a gestation period of only two weeks, up to 21 young may be born. At birth they are the size of a bean, blind, naked and poorly developed except for a single feature: the clawed front feet. With these claws the young pull themselves through the mother's fur to the pouch, where 13 of them will attach themselves to nipples and the rest will not survive. They remain in the pouch two months until their eyes open and they can emerge. The pouch is a traveling nursery for some time, however.

The opossum's diet may be one reason for its tenacious existence. Nearly as omnivorous as the coyote, the opossum eats rodents, insects, worms, birds, eggs, meat, fruit and berries. Not well adapted to a desert life, the opossum stays near river bottoms where it can be near water.

The opossum's powerful jaws are studded with 50 teeth, more than any mammal native to the United States. Although formidable weapons, the teeth are rarely used when the opossum is faced with danger. Instead, it will run to cover, or if unable to run will "play opossum," or feign death. Its heartbeat slows, muscles become limp and reflexes are dulled. Although it appears lifeless, it will come out of the trance if left alone.

RANGE: The Lower Sonoran Zone of west Texas east of the Pecos River and parts of northern Mexico.

HABITAT: Brushy or wooded stream bottoms.

ARMADILLO
Dasypus novemcinctus

DESCRIPTION: The only mammal with its body encased in armor. Total length about 30 inches (75 centimeters), tail about 14 inches (35 centimeters). Skin of upper body and back modified into a semi-flexible bony shell. Center of top half of shell circles across the back with nine rows of bony plates mounted on a flexible base allowing the body to curl into a ball. Front of face, top of head and outer surface of ears well protected with bony covering. Skin of underparts and sides of face tough and leathery. Teeth absent in fronts of upper and lower jaws. Teeth in the backs of the jaws are peglike.

These curious animals, evolutionary holdovers, are included here because they are definitely a part of the Southwest's fauna, although they are limited in their occurrence. In size, today's armadillos do not compare to the huge species that once roamed North and South America. Although not typical desert mammals, they can exist under arid conditions. They exist on the edges of the desert by moving about mainly at night, remaining underground in cool burrows during the heat of the day.

Members of the same group as the anteaters, armadillos are largely insectivorous. In their search for ants, earthworms, grubs, beetles, spiders and almost any kind of insect, they are aided by long claws and a pointed nose. The claws can rake and dig the earth and the nose can be used for rooting. They will also eat berries and fruits and have been accused of eating birds' eggs and young birds, but stomach content analyses have not confirmed this. Without front teeth, it is highly unlikely that they prey on mammals.

The nine-banded armadillos usually produce four or more young, all of the same sex in a litter. The unisexual litters occur because all the young develop from one egg, a phenomenon rare in the animal world. This may help the continuation of the species, but it is not certain what purpose it actually serves.

The young are born in burrows dug in soft soil. At birth they are covered with a soft skin resembling thin leather, which gradually changes to the bony covering of the adult.

The armadillo's armor may at one time have been more effective than presently appears. When the armadillo curls into its defensive posture, the sides of the body are vulnerable to attack because the armor is less heavy and more easily breached.

RANGE: Well distributed through northern South America and Mexico, penetrating into the United States mainly in southwest Texas and possibly southeastern New Mexico.

HABITAT: Brush areas with soft loamy or sandy soils.

DESERT MULE DEER
Odocoileus hemionus crooki

DESCRIPTION: A large gray deer with a black-tipped tail. Upper parts dark gray with a darker stripe along back. Backs of legs grading into pale cinnamon. Underparts and middle of tail white. Antlers heavy and remarkably long along the beam before forking. The large ears give this species its name, *hemionus,* or "burro." Weight of an average adult buck is 150 pounds (67.5 kilograms). One or two fawns born in early summer.

These desert relatives of the mule deer of the Rocky Mountains have been declining since the 1960s. In Arizona, where they once lived mainly in the foothills, they occupy the lower desert, hiding among the mesquites and ironwoods in close association with the peccaries. In New Mexico where the low, dry plains are devoid of trees they live mostly in the oaks of the Upper Sonoran Zone, at times penetrating into the barren valleys. Their decline may be part of a natural cycle, although biologists have offered several other reasons, including overharvesting, range reduction, habitat changes from livestock, increases in deer population, poor reproduction, and other human-caused changes.

Easily distinguished from the Sonora white-tailed deer, mule deer have a short-haired tail tipped with black and large, wide ears. In addition, the mature mule deer bucks have characteristic antlers—widespread and heavy with few points. The measurement between the burr (the flare at the base of the horn where it is attached to the skull) and the first fork is greater than that of any other native southwestern deer.

The desert mule deer is most active at night. During the heat of the day it retires under the shade of a large rock or in the washes under a mesquite, where it will remain motionless for hours save for the flicking movement of its ears.

By late afternoon the deer will leave its shelter to find water in a spring or tank. It may dig a shallow hole in a wash to find a natural dam a few feet beneath the surface.

After drinking, the animal begins searching for food. These deer are browsers, preferring leaves and twigs of shrubs and trees to grass. They nibble a twig or two on one shrub, then move to the next, leaving little sign that they have eaten. This constant seemingly aimless wandering makes them less of a target for predators than if they followed a definite trail or stayed in one place.

In addition to its favored browse, deer will eat cactus and jojoba fruits and some grass. Their sensitive lips allow them to strip leaves from a spiny plant without encountering the plant's defense.

In flight the desert mule deer bounds through rough broken country with ease. Other than flight, its best defense is coloration.

Both bucks and does employ their sharp hoofs as weapons. In the spring the female will paw at the yearling fawn as it attempts to stay near her. They apparently tire of this harsh treatment and leave their mother.

Newborn fawns are hidden until they are large enough to follow their mothers. If a

fawn appears lost, it probably is not; the mother undoubtedly knows where it is and will find it if it is moved or frightened away.

RANGE: Southern Arizona, southern New Mexico, and southern Texas.

HABITAT: Desert foothills among low scrub growth or in thick growth along washes.

SONORA WHITE-TAILED DEER
Odocoileus virginianus couesi

DESCRIPTION: A small, gray deer with a large white tail. Total length about 60 inches (150 centimeters), tail about 13 inches (32.5 centimeters). Weight, 100 pounds (45 kilograms) or less. Color gray, relieved by touches of brown to cinnamon on legs. Belly and inner surface of hind legs white. Tail long and broad, lower surface pure white, upper surface gray to cinnamon with a white edging. Ears large, whitish on inner surface, gray on back. Antlers small but stout, curved sharply forward. Young, one or two, reddish spotted with white, later reddish gray until second year.

This small, shy deer is protected by its rough wooded habitat and is still present in some numbers in the higher mountains of its range. It has virtually disappeared from the lower canyons. The population is now divided between the Upper Sonoran and Transition zones, moving with the seasons. The winter snows drive the deer to the lower oaks of the Upper Sonoran Zone; the following summer many ascend to the aspen groves on the northern slopes of the higher peaks. After losing their antlers in the spring, mature bucks band together on the isolated summits.

The males of all southwest deer bear antlers. The first are simple curved tines, "spikes," which appear usually during the second year. After these are shed at the end of a year, they are replaced by a larger pair, each with a forked end. Every year the antlers increase in spread and points until a limit is reached. A buck may lose his antlers singly or both at the same time. New antlers then appear, bulbous, fuzzy growths that are covered with "velvet," a membrane filled with blood vessels and nerves. When the "rack" is fully grown the "velvet" dries up and is shed, often with the help of the buck rubbing his antlers against trees or posts.

In the fall the bucks fight for dominance in the herd. The victors each gather several does together and separate into family groups. After breeding these families remain together until spring. Fawns, usually one, but sometimes twins are born in June or July.

The Sonora white-tailed deer, although considered a browser, varies a diet of leaves and twigs with grass and herbs. Another item eaten in the fall is acorns of the Arizona white oaks.

The Sonora white-tail is a nervous, alert animal which when startled will hoist its tail and run swiftly from danger. It does not bound as the mule deer does.

RANGE: Southern Arizona and southern New Mexico.
HABITAT: Rough, wooded higher mountains.

14

DESERT BIGHORN SHEEP

Ovis canadensis mexicana

DESCRIPTION: A pale, brownish-gray sheep with heavy, curving horns in the male. Average length of an adult ram about 50 inches (125 centimeters), tail about 5 inches (12.5 centimeters), weight 150 to 200 pounds (67.5 to 90 kilograms). Females weigh from 75 to 115 pounds (33.8 to 51.8 kilograms). General body color is buff gray with a darker line along the middle of the back. Cloven hoofs. The prominent eyes are a beautiful hazel-amber color. Both sexes are horned, the female's slimmer and shorter than the massive, curved horns of the male.

The Spanish explorer Coronado reported seeing bighorn in 1540 and in 1697 Jesuit missionaries recorded it in Baja California. Hunting, diseases and intrusions on their territories have diminished bighorn numbers, and now in many places only scattered bands remain. In many locations these remnant populations have retreated to inaccessible mountainous areas. Many states are conducting transplant operations to reestablish bighorn in former ranges.

Bighorn depend more on water than many desert creatures; in fact, water is the most limiting environmental factor of bighorn populations. One of the best places to observe bighorn is at a spring or natural rock tank. On hot, dry summer days they drink at least once daily, usually in the early mornings. Bighorn have been reported to go without water from 5-8 days however.

Adaptations to climate have produced noticeable differences in desert bighorn. The coat is scanty and harsher than that of the northern species, making the neck look thinner and the head proportionately larger. The pelage is drabber, and the brown areas are paler. The white rump patch is smaller and shades into brown rather than being distinctly white. Desert bighorn are much smaller in size than the northern species.

One of the bighorn's keys to survival is its ability to escape in rough, sometimes vertical terrain. Its cloven hoofs, flinty and hard with rough resilient undersurfaces, assure this ability. The concave hollow near the tip of the hoof gives the sheep footholds on minute rock projections, cushions their leaps, and allows them to jump 20 feet (6 meters) down onto another edge of the cliff face.

The majestic curved horns of the male are formed from a bony structure in their base, the horn core. The horn material, keratin, is pushed out from the skull. Annual growth is marked by a slight indentation around the horn, forming a ring that is noticeable even at some distance. These annual growth rings can be helpful in determining a sheep's age. Ordinarily it takes about 10 years for the horn to reach full growth, although growth continues throughout the bighorn's life. Actual horn length may decrease because of "brooming," in which the horn tips become worn and broken from abrasion against rocks and dirt or from butting heads with other rams during rut.

Their ability to escape has allowed bighorn to be largely free from predatory

pressure. An occasional kill has been reported, but no large predators depend on the bighorn.

During most of the year the rams and ewes roam separately. Each group is led by an animal of physical superiority, which stands watch and signals approaching danger by snorting and flashing its rump patch. In late summer and early fall breeding season arrives and the groups join. They battle to determine which shall lead the flock. Eventually several of the strongest rams may divide the ewes among them until the breeding is over.

Both a grazer and browser, the desert bighorn has little difficulty obtaining food, but a wide range of habitat is required so the necessary foods can be found at the right times. Bighorn eat succulent grasses that grow after rains as well as the leaves of desert shrubs. In addition, they will eat cactus, jojoba nuts and the fruiting heads of brittlebush.

RANGE: Deserts of California, Arizona, New Mexico, Texas, northern Mexico and Baja California.

HABITAT: Rocky ridges and higher pinnacles in mountainous and canyon-cut country. Lower and Upper Sonoran zones.

PRONGHORN
Antilocapra americana

DESCRIPTION: Smaller than a deer, buff with black markings on face, black horns with a single prong on each. Total length about 4.5 feet (1.35 meters), tail about 3 to 6 inches (7.5 to 15 centimeters). General color buff with white underparts, black strips on face and neck, and prominent white rump patch. Horns less than a foot (.3 meters) long with a single flat prong extending toward the front. Black cloven hoofs. Young, usually two, born in May.

The name antelope has erroneously been applied to this animal. True antelope are found only in the Old World. One of the physical differences that separates them is the horn structure. True antelope do not shed their horns, but add to their growth each year. The pronghorn's horn has a hollow core upon which the horn develops as a sort of sheath. This sheath is dropped during the fall and is replaced during the following season. Pronghorn are known for their speed, and have been clocked at 40 miles per hour (64 kilometers per hour). They tire quickly after short sprints, however.

Pronghorn are gregarious, roaming in bands of as few as a dozen to several hundred individuals. They are also highly polygamous. Early in the fall the males engage in fierce battles to determine the division of does. The vanquished males are driven out of the bands until breeding has occurred. The horns are soon shed, and with this loss the bucks also lose much of their former arrogance and the banished males are allowed to return.

Pronghorn populations in North America were formerly great, but reached a record low of 13,000 animals in the 1920s. Market hunting, railroads, highways, livestock competition, ranching and other human developments spelled their demise. However, their population has made a comeback with regulation of hunting, return of historical range and habitat, and wildlife management practices. The Sonoran pronghorn, listed as endangered by the U.S. Fish and Wildlife Service, may never have been abundant. Most pronghorns seen in the Southwest today are transplants from the north.

RANGE: Native to many parts of the West. The subspecies *mexicana* and *sonoriensis* in southern New Mexico and Arizona are now rare.

HABITAT: Grasslands of open valleys and mesas.

JAGUAR
Felis onca

DESCRIPTION: A huge yellow cat with black spots. Total length up to 8 feet (2.4 meters), tail about 30 inches (75 centimeters). Weight 250 pounds (112.5 kilograms) and more; muscular with heavy neck and broad, rounded face. General color tan to yellow, broken with dark rosettes which show much variation. The rosettes usually have a black center surrounded by a lighter area bordered by a black line. On the back the rosettes often merge into an irregular black median line extending from the shoulders to the tail. Underparts light yellow to gray with large solid black spots. Melanistic individuals, sometimes entirely black, are recorded in the tropics. Breeding habits are not well known, but presumably are similar to those of the mountain lion.

Jaguars are often mistakenly called leopards. Leopards, natives of the Old World, have spots instead of rosettes and are slim rather than heavy like jaguars.

The largest member of the cat family native to the Americas, the jaguar has an unearned reputation for ferocity. From accounts of the first Spanish explorers, it would seem that jaguars were common in parts of the Southwest. At that time it was probably native to this country but was soon eliminated as the land became settled. Any seen today presumably have come north from Mexico. The most northern records are at Grand Canyon in Arizona and near Santa Fe, New Mexico. South of these points they are reported in increasingly greater numbers, especially along mountain ranges linked with others in Mexico. The semi-tropical areas of southern Texas provide suitable country in which to enter, and many individuals have been recorded there.

Why the jaguar leaves the humid tropics for the desert is unclear. Its pattern of spots provides excellent camouflage in the light and shadow of the jungle and only make the jaguar conspicuous in the northern range. Prey is relatively scarce and there is little water. The jaguar is an inhabitant of river banks and hunts for food there and swims in waterholes.

Like the mountain lion the jaguar does not depend on speed to capture its prey. Instead, it will crouch on a limb overhanging a game trail and wait until suitable prey passes. With a spring it drops on the animal's back and takes it to the ground under its great weight. In brushy country devoid of trees the jaguar will slowly creep up on game, catching it and devouring it immediately.

Its preferred prey is peccaries and the jaguar's former range in the Southwest coincided with that of the peccary. In northwest Mexico it takes mountain sheep and deer, and occasionally domestic animals.

RANGE: The southern parts of Texas, New Mexico and Arizona; south through Mexico as far as Argentina in South America.

HABITAT: All three major life zones in the Southwest.

Mountain Lion
Felis concolor

DESCRIPTION: A large cat with a long, round tail. Total average length 6 to 7 feet (1.8 to 2.1 meters), tail 2 to 3 feet (.6 to .9 meters), weight from 100 to 200 pounds (45 to

90 kilograms). Grayish brown to brown in color with lighter areas under belly and insides of legs. Face with lighter markings around mouth bordered by a dark line. A powerfully built animal with a long, lean body and stout legs of medium length. Head small but broad, with short rounded ears and typical yellow-green cat's eyes. The feet are large and round, with sharp-clawed toes. Second only to the jaguar in size among native cats. The mountain lion's smooth coloration distinguishes it from the spotted black and yellow jaguar. Young, two to five, born primarily in late winter and early spring.

This animal's range once exceeded that of any American mammal. It extended from the northern United States to the southern end of South America, from the Atlantic to Pacific oceans. Except for rare sightings in Florida and a few other areas, it is no longer found in the eastern United States. It is still present in the western states. While usually called the mountain lion in the Southwest, this cat has been given many common names: cougar, catamount, puma and panther.

Although several varieties are recognized,the mountain lions of the two Americas belong to the same species. Their different environments give rise to varying habits, but generally their appearance is similar. Southwestern lions are paler and smaller than those living in the high mountains of the north or the thick tropical jungles. The mountain lion is predominantly nocturnal, but it will hunt in the day if prey are scarce. Males are solitary and secretive and require large territories. They often place scent marks, "scrapes" of dirt and needles and twigs in mounds on which they often urinate, to mark their territory.

This cat's favored food is deer, and it is estimated that a lion will kill one or two deer a week. When a lion moves into an area where deer are present, it first strikes those that are easiest to catch. After locating its prey it creeps up on it. When close enough to capture it, the lion makes several tremendous bounds landing with its full weight and clutching its claws on the deer's forequarters. It attempts to sink its teeth into the deer's neck to snap the bone or tear out the jugular. The first impact usually knocks the deer off its feet, and few escape.

Attacks may also be made from trees, where the lion's long hind legs allow it to leap at least 20 feet (6 meters).

After the kill is made, the lion usually drags the carcass to a secluded spot to eat it. When satiated, the lion covers the remaining meat with leaves and soil and may return several days later to finish it.

In addition to deer, the lion eats rodents, rabbits, porcupines, peccaries, bighorn sheep and any large game birds it can capture. It may also prey on domestic animals, especially horses.

Mating may take place any time of year, followed by a gestation of 90-96 days. Lion cubs are spotted with dark blotches when young, but the spots disappear when the young are three-fourths grown.

RANGE: In all states in the Southwest.

HABITAT: Upper Sonoran and Transition zones, but often descending to the Lower Sonoran Zone; lives on edge of rimrock country, where scrub desert ends and forest begins.

BOBCAT
Felis rufus

DESCRIPTION: Larger than a domestic cat. Tail is short and ears have short tufts at the tip. Total length 30 to 36 inches (75 to 90 centimeters), tail only about 5 inches (12.5 centimeters). These large cats weigh from 15 to 40 pounds (6.75 to 18 kilograms). Summer coat yellowish tan with scattered dark spots and usually several black "tiger" stripes. The thick winter coat is yellowish gray with the same black markings. Tail with white tip. Face similar to the domestic cat with characteristic long whiskers. Eyes yellow-green. Young, two to four, born in spring or summer.

Of the five species of the cat family recorded in the Southwest, the bobcat is the most common. It is smaller than the jaguar, mountain lion, and ocelot and about the same size as the jaguarundi, an animal so rare and different that it will not be confused with the bobcat. Although small, the bobcat has many characteristics common to its larger relatives, among them a timidity toward humans.

Although chiefly nocturnal, the bobcat will prowl by day. Ordinarily it spends days in a well-hidden retreat among rocks or in brushy thickets. Because it is shy and seldom seen, bobcats are believed to be rarer than they actually are in some locations. If approached by a human while resting, it will borrow a trick from the rabbits and lie perfectly motionless, depending on its protective coloration to escape detection. If routed from its resting place, it will run to the nearest cover with a bobbing, rather awkward gait. Although capable of speed for short distances, it will soon tire.

This lack of endurance is reflected in its hunting habits: the bobcat normally captures prey through stealth rather than pursuit, crouching in wait beside a rabbit trail to make a capture. Its keen eyes, ears and claws make the bobcat a formidable predator to the small animals and birds that it hunts. Though its food is chiefly cottontails, jackrabbits, and small rodents, it will occasionally kill young deer and pronghorn and ground nesting birds. Like most predators, it also catches numerous insects. Strangely, although at home in the trees, the bobcat spends little time aloft. The belief that it preys on cattle and the value of its pelt have led to declining bobcat populations in some areas.

Bobcats normally bear only one litter each year. For the first few weeks, the young, usually two to four in number, greatly resemble the kittens of a domestic cat. The general color and markings are not unlike those of a "tiger stripe," and the stubby tail is also present at birth. Kittens of all species of the cat family are born blind. Shortly after a bobcat kitten's eyes open, other changes gradually become apparent. Most noticeable are the round faces, heavy legs and large feet. At six weeks, the play instinct is fully developed. When awake, the family will wrestle and play for hours. At other times more serious encounters develop, when mother brings home a small animal. Then each kitten attempts to capture the entire prize by any method possible. The male bobcat takes no part in providing for the family; in fact, he is driven from the vicinity of the den by the mother. Male bobcats have been known

to kill the young, a habit especially pronounced in the cat family. By the time they are half grown, the kittens are able to leave the den for nightly forays with the mother as they develop their hunting instincts.

Occasionally bobcats are among the noisiest animals in the desert. The cries of a male bobcat at mating time are a familiar back-alley type howl.

In spring or early summer the female finds a den, preferably in a cavity deep among the rocks. If this is not available, she will select a hollow log, or less often, a nest under tangled brush. Little provision is made for the comfort of the young. The floor of the den is smoothed off, and in these dens the young are born.

RANGE: Desert areas of New Mexico, Nevada, Arizona, California, Texas and northern Mexico.

HABITAT: Rough, broken terrain, principally in the Upper Sonoran Zone, but also found in the Lower Sonoran and Transition zones.

GRAY WOLF
Canis lupus

DESCRIPTION: Several formerly well-defined varieties have crossbred to produce a mixture of races, thus permitting only a few of the more typical characteristics to be given. The gray wolf is a large animal that resembles a large German shepherd dog. Total length about 5.5 feet (1.65 meters), tail about 18 inches (45 centimeters). Heavy through neck and shoulders. Fully matured, will weigh from 60 to more than 100 pounds (27 to 45 kilograms). Fur is coarse and long, especially around the neck. Head broad with comparatively short ears, nose short and wide. Tail, also rather short, is brushy. Young, from two to 12, born in early spring.

Color may range from slate blue, brown, cinnamon gray and blond to white.

Wolves move about eight to ten hours a day, traveling great distances searching for food. Packs, once containing many individuals, are now usually limited to only a few. They are typically dominated by one male and one female. The social organization of the pack is closely intertwined with all the wolf's activities—breeding, hunting, and communication. The size of litters will depend on this social organization and determination of which males and females will breed. Wolves mate for life, breeding normally in February and March each year. Young are born in April and May, and weaned in five weeks.

Dens are built in natural cavities around boulders, caves, or in burrows in a well-concealed location. Mortality among the pups is high: more than half may die from disease, starvation or other factors.

Wolves communicate within their own pack and with other packs by vocalizations (howls, growls, squeaks), posturing and scent-marking. By urinating on objects and on the ground they mark their territorial boundaries, and these boundaries are quickly detected by pups or other adult wolves.

Wolves prefer meat of larger animals such as elk, moose, and caribou but will also eat mice, squirrels and rabbits. The wolf's powerful jaws and sharp teeth are especially adapted for the kind of prey on which it lives. In the West their primary food source historically was the buffalo. When the buffalo herds were exterminated, wolves turned to cattle or whatever else they could find. Vigorous predator control campaigns in the early 1900s virtually eliminated wolves that lived in the Southwest.

RANGE: Once found on most of the prairie lands of the West.

HABITAT: Prefer better browse and grassland areas where chief prey, ungulates, live. Upper Sonoran to Hudsonian zones.

COYOTE
Canis latrans

DESCRIPTION: Larger than a fox, but smaller than a wolf, the coyote may weigh 20-50 pounds (9-22.5 kilograms), measure 32-37 inches (80-92.5 centimeters) and its tail is 11-16 inches (27.5-40 centimeters). Looks much like a medium-sized dog, but the nose is more pointed and the tail is bushier. Many subspecies, all closely resembling one another.

The female coyote anxiously guards the pups and will move them if she senses that the den has been discovered. While small, the pups milk diet is supplemented by solid food eaten by the parents and regurgitated. Shortly before they leave the den the young are brought whole animals and birds. Tearing apart this food strengthens the young coyotes' jaws and muscles preparing them to accompany the parents on hunts.

The coyote is a predator, scavenger and vegetarian and can exist under almost any conditions. As predator it eliminates primarily the old, weak or diseased animals especially among elk, deer and pronghorn, thus removing the individuals that tend to impair a species vitality. Coyotes effectively control numbers of smaller mammals, especially rodents.

As scavengers, coyotes dispose of the remains of dead animals, many of which they find along highways. As a vegetarian, the coyote is highly versatile—it will eat melons, dates, juniper berries and succulent roots and occasionally grass.

The coyote's scientific name, *Canis latrans,* means barking dog, a name it has earned because of its varied vocalizations. A wide-ranging repertoire of barks, yips, yelps and growls have been recorded and are believed to be a communications network among coyotes.

Subject of many native American legends, the coyote was generally considered a dupe, sometimes a creator, ranked as something of a deity. J. Frank Dobie, author of the classic book, *The Voice of the Coyote,* records the find of an ancient bowl from northern Mexico which bore the symbol of a coyote head on one side and a badger head on the other. A strange association has been observed between these two animals, in which the coyote shares part of its catch with the badger while the badger repays by frightening rodents from their burrows to a waiting coyote.

Coyotes have been the targets of many predator control programs in the West, because of complaints that they kill domestic sheep. Much controversy surrounds the control methods, but coyotes have been remarkably able to adapt to these attacks and have multiplied in numbers.

RANGE: Perhaps the most widespread mammal in the United States presently. Once an inhabitant of only the western prairies, it has now been recorded in almost all states. The coyote is common through the West, especially in the Southwest.

HABITAT: At home in almost any kind of climate and every type of terrain. Has been found in all life zones except possibly Alpine.

GRAY FOX

Urocyon cinereoargenteus

DESCRIPTION: Small, total length about 40 inches (100 centimeters), tail 18 inches (45 centimeters) long. Can be recognized by gray color above and orange or reddish sides and throat. Underparts lighter gray. Large, bushy tail with a black tip. Average weight from 10 to 18 pounds (4.5 to 8.1 kilograms). The three or four young are born in early spring.

The gray fox's large ears, graceful bearing and large bushy tail clearly identify it as a member of the fox clan. However, it is often confused with the red fox due to its definite reddish orange coloration on the sides and throat.

Its keen intelligence has allowed it to maintain its numbers in the face of encroaching civilization. These animals are often found within city limits, wherever weedy or brushy areas offer sufficient cover.

In the open areas they prefer, they are free-ranging animals that hunt widely. Like coyotes, they tend to travel the same paths nightly. Although these foxes prefer a diet of rodents, they by no means depend on them solely. Other small mammals, birds and bird eggs, amphibians, and some reptiles are consumed. Almost as omnivorous as the coyote and the bear, these desert foxes do not hesitate to adopt a vegetarian diet at times. Berries, wild dates, cactus fruits and several kinds of tubers are eaten, providing nourishment when other favored foods are unavailable. This indiscriminate appetite allows the gray fox to live where predators with more specific needs could not.

The fox has adopted several unusual hunting techniques. Although a member of the Canidae or dog family, it has developed some habits more characteristic of the cats. Lacking a coyote's speed, the fox is more likely to sneak up on its prey. When pouncing on a rodent, the fox does not depend on its jaws alone; instead, it strikes its prey in a catlike manner, with both paws, to pin it to the ground. Like the cats, it is a master of the ambush and will crouch motionless for hours if necessary along a rabbit trail waiting for its victim. Surprisingly, many foxes are good climbers, and this species is one of the most adept. It does not hesitate to take to the trees to escape or search for food. It has been known to den in hollow trees, sometimes far above the ground. However, usually the dens are in deep burrows or in rocky clefts.

The gray fox is far more active at night than in the day. Its bark or yap, similar to that of a small dog, can be heard at night. Other sounds it emits are so foreign that one would never suspect that a fox is making them. If caught in a flashlight's beam, this fox's eyes glow a brilliant yellow-green, allowing reasonably certain identification even if the body outlines are not visible. In the lower desert, this particular trait is shared with the kit fox.

In winter gray foxes descend along the canyons into the warmer areas; with the return of summer they retreat to the higher altitudes. It is not unusual to encounter them in the Transition Zone in this season. The annual movements of many southwestern mammals are like those of migrating birds in that the object is to maintain a favorable climate. Birds, of course, can fly long distances, while mammals move up and down mountainsides.

RANGE: Common in New Mexico, Arizona, Texas and California.

HABITAT: Upper Sonoran Zone, but also common in the Lower Sonoran and Transition zones. Canyons and rough country provide ideal locations for dens and concealment.

KIT FOX
Vulpes macrotis

DESCRIPTION: Small size with exceptionally large ears. West of the Rio Grande River, the kit fox, *V. macrotis,* is the common form. East of this river the species is more likely to *V. velox,* the swift fox, or "prairie swift." Both species are similar in appearance and habits. Total length about 30 inches (75 centimeters), tail about 12 inches (30 centimeters), color yellowish gray above, shading to buff along the sides and lower surface of the tail. Underparts lighter buff, with white under throat and posterior part of belly. The tail is tipped with black. An adult may weigh approximately 5 pounds (2.25 kilograms). Young, three or four, born in early spring.

The diminutive size of this, the smallest member of the canine family in the U.S., is surprising. It is not especially rare or timid, those who roam the desert have likely seen one.

The kit fox inhabits the lowest levels of every region in which it is found. In New Mexico this may include part of the Upper Sonoran Zone, but in Arizona and California its range will be chiefly Lower Sonoran. Here it prefers the wide alluvial plains adjacent to the Mexican boundary from the Rio Grande to the Coastal Range in California. In this sparsely populated region it is associated with the various species of kangaroo rats of the genus *Dipodomys,* more than with any other animal. Like some of the kangaroo rats, the kit fox has developed hairs under the feet that enable it to run over the soft sand and loose soils more easily. It is interesting to note that most animals which live in this type habitat have developed such adaptations. This includes lizards, some of which have developed fringes along the toes for better footing.

The canid family is a notable exception in the ranks of the mammals in that males take an active part in raising young. The male kit fox is exemplary in his devotion to his mate and his zeal in bringing small game home for the family. This task begins when the young are being weaned and lasts, with increasing demands, until the young can leave the den. During this period, if the female is not present, the male can raise the family alone.

The den of the kit fox is usually found in alluvial soil under a mound of excavated earth designed to prevent flooding. Many have several entrances. Some dens are apparently merely enlarged and remodeled kangaroo rat dens. As a rule the burrow is dug at a steep angle and levels off about 2 feet (.6 meters) under the surface. The auxiliary entrances join this main tunnel rather than the den itself.

Their catlike agility and swiftness makes these small foxes adept at catching rodents, their chief food. Even the erratic flight of the kangaroo rats is not proof against their speed.

RANGE: Arizona, Nevada, New Mexico and southern California.

HABITAT: Lower Sonoran Zone. Mesas and valleys of the low desert country, often in brushy but not necessarily rocky locations. Its home is a burrow, usually with several entrances in alluvial soil.

DALE C. THOMPSON

MEXICAN RACCOON

Procyon lotor mexicanus

DESCRIPTION: A black mask and ringed tail are two outstanding characteristics that identify this animal. Total length about 35 inches (87.5 centimeters), tail about 12 inches (30 centimeters). General color gray with a black mask, the brushy tail encircled with five or six black bands. Face broad with a pointed nose. Build broad and low, legs short, feet plantigrade (the sole of the foot is flat with the heel meeting the ground, as with bears and men), front feet with long toes, those of hind feet shorter. Young, four to six, born any time of year. Paler than the eastern raccoon.

Much of what is called desert in the Southwest consists of broad, almost flat valleys at elevations that place them in the Lower or Upper Sonoran Zone. Between them are mountains which often rise into the Transition Zone and sometimes above it. Enough precipitation falls on these mountains to form small streams, flowing year-round. Along these streams a luxuriant growth of trees and underbrush creates protection for a host of animals, among them the raccoon. Accustomed to running water, this animal will not venture far from this favored habitat; thus, its distribution is spotty throughout the desert region. Although bound to canyons by water requirements, the raccoon can follow a streamcourse and frequently ascend to the source which may be in the pines of the Transition Zone. This usually happens in the summer, otherwise the raccoon prefers the relative warmth of the lower parts of canyons during the winter.

Eastern raccoons almost invariably den in hollow trees, usually high above ground. The Mexican raccoon also dens in trees whenever possible, but if suitable trees are not available it will den in a pile of rocks or in a small cave. Sometimes it takes advantage of a deep crevice in a cliff in which to rear young, which mature rapidly and are soon able to hunt on their own. They commonly share the den, however, until they are fully mature, even though this makes for crowded quarters. While young raccoons may make intelligent, mischievous pets, as with all wild animals it is best to allow them to live in their natural habitat where they can fully take care of themselves.

Raccoons have remarkable feet which are responsible for some of the animal's unique habits. First cousins to the bears, raccoons have a rolling gait reminiscent of that huge animal. This walk is due to the plantigrade feet that both species possess. The bear, though handy with its front feet, cannot begin to match the raccoon's dexterity. They wash food, grasp small branches while climbing, hunt for crayfish, open mussels, strip husks from ears of corn, pick fruit and nuts, and engage in numerous other activities. Few sights are more amusing than an old raccoon, crouched by the edge of a pool looking vacantly into space, while its fingers are busily exploring every nook and cranny under the bank for a frog.

The raccoon's track is distinctive. Somewhat like a child's footprint in outline, it can be found in the soft mud along streams. The coati's track resembles it but is longer and shows long claws on the forefeet. Some skunks also make roughly similar tracks.

Few animals are more omnivorous than raccoons. First preference is food found in or near water, including shellfish, crawfish, frogs and an occasional small fish. Small piles of shells are often a sign that a raccoon has been eating on a rock, opening and washing its catch. The most important vegetable food is mesquite beans, which may be eaten exclusively in autumn. Acorns, berries, and cactus fruits are taken whenever available. Rodents and other small game are perhaps the most insignificant part of the menu when other foods are readily at hand.

RANGE: In all the southwestern states.

HABITAT: In the Lower and Upper Sonoran and Transition zones. Rough canyons and brushy bottoms near running water.

COATI
Nasua ŋasua

DESCRIPTION: A medium-sized, rusty brown animal with a long tail and piglike snout. Total length about 4 feet (1.2 meters), tail about 2 feet (.6 meters). Tail bushy and ringed with some 10 dark and 10 light rings. General body color is honey to rusty brown with a dark mask across the face. Lighter spots above and below the eyes. Nose long and flexible and terminating with a pig like pad of gristle. Feet plantigrade, that is the weight is distributed between sole and toes as with the human foot. Front feet armed with powerful, long claws; those on hind feet shorter. The short, rounded ears are close to the skull. Young, three or more, born in early summer. Type of den unknown to this writer but presumed to be in burrows among the rocks or, in some cases, nests in hollow trees.

The coati's migration from Mexico into the U.S. is one of the rare cases in which a foreign species has been added through natural invasion rather than artificial. Why they crossed the wide valleys that separate most of the mountain ranges from Mexico is an enigma. Whether they will remain in the area, migrate farther north, or retreat to their former range is also uncertain.

The first scientific records of their presence in the U.S. were written in the 1920s and 1930s on specimens collected near the border. However, eyewitness accounts by ranchers established that they were in the Rincon Mountains in what is now part of the Saguaro National Monument in the early 1900s.

The coati's appearance suggests a mixture of several better known mammals. The tip of the nose, although smaller, is much the same shape as the javelina's and has the same function: rooting among the leaves and loam in search of insects and tuberous roots. The face is long and narrow, yet the dark mask is strikingly reminiscent of the badger. The impression is heightened by the short, round ears. The coati's ears are constructed so that when they are laid against the head, a tuft of long, coarse hair folds across the opening to the inner ear, sealing out dirt and loam.

Its slim jaws are lined with long, sharp teeth, the canines being an inch or more long in adults. The small, soft, brown eyes belie this weaponry and instead lend a wistful expression to the coati's unusual face. The coati's body is long and flat-sided, and the legs are medium length. The feet have long narrow soles that leave a characteristic track. The hind feet are much longer than the front feet, but have shorter claws. The hind feet are responsible for the shuffling, loose gait of the coati that resembles that of the black bear.

The tail, about as long as the body, is usually carried upright with the hair standing at right angles. In the sun the darker bands can be clearly distinguished, but in the shade they are inconspicuous. Coatis are sometimes mistaken for monkeys because of their long tails, but their tails are not prehensile. However, they are used as props when the animal stands on its hind legs to reach a low-hanging object.

In Arizona two types of coatis are found: a typical rusty brown animal with a bushy, indistinctly-banded tail and a much, darker almost black animal, with a tail smoothly furred and unbanded. The only specimens of the latter type that this writer has encountered are old males, and it is highly probable that these are melanistic (dark color variation) phases of the same species.

Coatis are highly gregarious, roaming the woodlands in groups of several to as many as 20 members. Sometimes they travel in single file, but more often they are in a scattered formation, searching for food. The females retire from the band to bear young, but as soon as they are old enough to travel the family joins the nearest group. Several females often travel together with their families, and may care for each other's young.

The young add confusion to the band because they frequently wander away and become disoriented. Even within a short distance of their mother, they send out high, piping calls answered with a series of worried grunts from the mother until the "lost" young is found.

Little is known about the regimen of their community life, but occasionally an old male is found that never travels with the band. Whether they are outcasts or merely individualists is unknown. The Mexicans have given them a special name, *solitarios,* the solitary ones.

Like their closest relatives the raccoons, the coatis can be considered omnivorous. The staple diet throughout the year is small rodents, worms, insects and tubers unearthed from beds of leaves and soft loam. It is varied in season by juniper and manzanita berries, other small fruits, bird eggs, young birds and whatever small mammals come their way. In the writer's experience, coatis have not been seen actively hunting and stalking other mammals and birds. Rather, they catch prey when the opportunity arises during their search for insects and plants.

The coati is marvelously adapted to making its living. The long hind feet, looking like they've been "turned under," form a solid base that bears the animal's weight as it crouches close to the ground. The tail balances the weight as the nose and long front claws winnow through the leaf mold. Worms and crawling insects are rooted out by the specially adapted nose, and flying insects are batted down or caught between the front paws. The front claws are used to overturn large rocks, where lizards and small snakes may also be found.

Coatis are equally at home in trees. At the first indication of danger, a coati will freeze to evade discovery. Failing this, it will dash for the nearest tree and scamper up the trunk like a cat. They are able to descend headfirst or tailfirst.

This climbing ability compensates for the coati's slow running speed. The writer once paced a coati with a car for 150 yards (135 meters), and the best speed the animal could attain was 17 miles per hour (27.2 kilometers per hour). The gait was a shambling gallop that soon exhausted the animal.

The coati has defenses other than that of flight. The sharp teeth and long claws render it a formidable adversary, especially if cornered. Coatis have few natural enemies, but when they become embroiled in battles with ranch dogs, they are usually victorious.

RANGE: Southern and central Arizona, southwest Texas, southwest New Mexico and Mexico.

HABITAT: Lower and Upper Sonoran and Transition zones. Brushy thickets and rocky locations.

RINGTAIL

Bassariscus astutus

DESCRIPTION: A small animal with large eyes and a tail ringed with black stripes. Total length about 30 inches (75 centimeters), tail about 15 inches (37.5 centimeters). The long, bushy tail is the most conspicuous feature of the animal. As long as the head and body combined, the tail is a beautiful combination of about seven black and seven white rings terminating in a black tip. General body color is buffy gray, face with a darker stripe on cheeks and over the eyes. The head and face have a foxlike look, except the eyes are more prominent and ears are rounded. The legs are short compared with the rather long body. Feet small and round, leaving tracks resembling those of a house cat.

The normally shy ringtail is another southwestern mammal about which comparatively little is known. They are widely distributed, ranging from as far north as Utah and southern Oregon through Mexico to Central America. In the southern portion of their range, they occur from near sea level to as high as 10000 feet (3000 meters). In the Southwest they mainly live in the Upper Sonoran Zone, but are often found in the brushy canyons that extend into the valleys of the Lower Sonoran Zone. In summer they are found in the Transition Zone, but comparatively few are year-round residents at that altitude.

They are known by many common names, most of them ending in ''cat''—miner's cat, band-tailed cat, civet cat and coon cat. Although these animals have many of the customary habits of cats, they are most closely related to the raccoons. They have little outward resemblance to these animals, except the bushy, ringed tail. The ringtail is a highly individualistic animal with habits peculiarly its own. Physically it may resemble many species, but can be directly compared to none.

The ringtail's favorite habitat is along the cliffs of the abrupt desert canyons. Their almost weasel-like bodies and short legs allow them to prowl ledges and crevices for prey. Dead leaves and branches that lodge in such places harbor many rodents and insects, eagerly taken by the ringtail. They can be considered strictly nocturnal animals, normally never seen in the daytime. They spend their days asleep in the semi-darkness of an overhanging ledge or in a hollow tree.

Ringtails are among the most active of the small predators. They often cover a considerable area several times a night, their silence often enabling them to catch a rodent that had evaded them. Although expert climbers, they spend little time off the ground, taking to the trees only to hunt roosting birds or their nests. Under natural conditions they rarely depart from their carnivorous and insectivorous diet. At times, fruits of the cactus and wild palms are eaten.

RANGE: In all of the southwestern states.

HABITAT: Usually in the Upper Sonoran Zone but often descending into the Lower Sonoran Zone. Prefers cliffs and rocky canyons in the oak belt, but is also found along the brushy arroyos in the lower desert, especially in winter.

BADGER
Taxidea taxus

DESCRIPTION: Conspicuously broad and heavy, with a flattened appearance. The legs are short, front feet are armed with stout claws up to 1.5 inches (3.75 centimeters) long; hind claws shorter. The coarse body hair is yellowish gray; hair on feet and face black, except for a white stripe along the cheeks. Another white stripe extends from the nose between the ears and terminates between the shoulders. Weight from 15 to 30 pounds (6.75 to 13.5 kilograms). Four or five young are born in early summer.

The badger is often mistaken for a large rodent because of its burrowing habits, but in fact it is a member of the weasel family. It possesses the irritability and predatory traits of that group. Weasels and badgers are related to skunks and all have glands producing scents that are offensive in varying degrees. The badger's scent, while not potent enough to give it the respect shown to a skunk, is highly repugnant. Despite its comparatively small size, the badger is liberally endowed with defenses and predators avoid it. The long, raking claws, sharp teeth and loose skin combine to allow it to defend itself against enemies. However, it is shy and would much rather retreat than fight. If left alone, it will go its way. If cornered, it growls and hisses menacingly and advances at once upon any threatening movement.

The badger's food is largely rodents, but it also preys on ground-dwelling birds and their eggs as well as various insects and reptiles. This low-slung burrower is especially valuable as a control on gophers, ground squirrels, and prairie dogs. If a few sniffs with its keen nose tells the badger that a ground squirrel is in a burrow, the badger will dig out the burrow until it is large enough to enter. These holes, whether dug in pursuit of a rodent or used as a den are typically wider than they are high, evidence that the badger has excavated them.

Unfortunately, these holes are the chief cause of the badger's extermination over most of its former range. Its benefit as a control on rodents has not been considered to outweigh the danger the burrows present to horses and cattles that may stumble in the holes and break a leg. Once common throughout the West from southern Canada to central Mexico, the badger is becoming increasingly rare in the U.S.

The badger is diurnal and nocturnal in its habits. It is frequently abroad in the mornings and late afternoons and occasionally during the middle of the day. Little is known of its life history, although it is suspected that it mates for life. They are solitary animals, and are seldom seen together except during the breeding season. Several cases, however, have been recorded of a badger and coyote traveling together.

RANGE: In all the southwestern states.

HABITAT: Occurs in all life zones, but most numerous in desert valleys of the Lower Sonoran Zone. Almost any type of terrain, but deep alluvial soil preferred where it will dig deep burrows or shallow holes.

BLACK-FOOTED FERRET
Mustela nigripes

DESCRIPTION: A large black-footed, black-masked weasel about the size of an eastern mink. Total length about 26 inches (65 centimeters), tail less than 3 inches (7.5 centimeters). General color buff or cream, darker along the middle of the back and lighter underneath. Feet and tip of tail are black as is a prominent mask across the face and eyes. Ears rather large. Lithe, sinewy body with short legs. Number of young unknown, but presumed to be from four to six.

One of the rarest western mammals, few people have seen a black-footed ferret and little is known of its life history. The black-footed ferret is a true native of the United States and once occupied a wide range of land in the Southwest and Midwest. With the conversion of most of its hunting grounds to agricultural and rangelands, it is now limited mainly to the grassy plains of the Southwest.

Black-footed ferrets are listed as endangered by the U.S. Fish and Wildlife Service.

This species illustrates well the dependence of one animal on another. The black-footed ferret has become specialized at catching prairie dogs, and in areas where the prairie dogs have been exterminated the ferrets have also disappeared.

These ferrets, like their smaller cousins the weasels, are bold and inquisitive. Like the weasels, they have a sinuous, flowing movement. If pursued, they will retreat to a safe position and then offer a defiance unusual in animals of their size.

They will glide down the entrance of a kangaroo rat mound and reappear quickly at another, giving the impression that there are several ferrets in one burrow. Although its preference for prairie dogs has been stressed, the black-footed ferret also captures smaller ground squirrels and other small rodents. It captures these above ground, because the burrows are too small to enter. Ferrets are active in the day and at night, but will most likely be seen in early morning or late afternoon.

Burrowing owls are often caught off-guard during the day in prairie dog burrows, and other ground-nesting birds fall easy prey to the ferret at night. A good climber, it can ascend low desert trees to reach a roosting bird.

RANGE: In the Southwest, Colorado and New Mexico; formerly from the southwestern states north as far as the Canadian border.

HABITAT: Mainly open plains, associated with prairie dog towns.

HOODED SKUNK
Mephitis macroura

DESCRIPTION: A small, slender skunk with a hood or cap of longer hairs, usually white, on neck and head. Total length 26 inches (65 centimeters), tail 14 inches (35 centimeters). Body is black with a white stripe down the back and top of the tail and another along each side. A white stripe is also present between the eyes. The fur including the hood, is long and soft. This species is extremely variable, with many deviations from the above pattern encountered. Melanistic phases are frequently reported in which the pelage is black except for the white stripe between the eyes. From three to five young are born in late spring in a den among the rocks or in a burrow dug in alluvial soil.

51

An expert hunter, the hooded skunk pursues rodents, small birds, and insects, thoroughly covering a territory on its nocturnal rounds. Beds of leaf mold are scratched, bases of shrubs and cholla dug around, and flat rocks turned over in search of insects. All likely hiding places of rodents are investigated as are clumps of grass which might shelter a bird nest. At dawn, skunks retire to a burrow or deep crevice among the rocks to sleep during the day.

Their noctural forays continue throughout the year, the hooded skunks being the most active of all skunks except the striped skunk. They are confined to their dens only rarely when it rains. Their nimbleness and boldness makes them interesting and amusing to observe. The young accompany the mother on evening food searches, and frequently the entire group engages in mock battles. Occasionally the skirmishes escalate to a baring of the teeth and claws, accompanied by a monkey-like sharp chittering cry.

RANGE: Southwestern New Mexico, southern Arizona, west Texas, northwestern Mexico.

HABITAT: Lower Sonoran Zone. Valleys and lower canyons in brushy or rocky situations.

STRIPED SKUNK
Mephitis mephitis

DESCRIPTION: A black and white animal slightly smaller than a cat. Total length 22 to 30 inches (55 to 75 centimeters), tail 8 to 15 inches (20 to 37.5 centimeters) in length. Body color black with a narrow white stripe down the center of the forehead; usually two white stripes down the back. The large bushy tail is mostly white in the average specimen. Number of young, four to six.

This common southwestern skunk is closely allied to the striped skunk of the northern United States. It may be assumed that any skunk seen in this range having two white stripes down the back will be this species.

This is the most plentiful of the four species of desert skunks, and can be expected in any locality that offers suitable denning habitat. Dens may be burrows dug in soft soil or in crevices among rock slides. The striped skunk does not depend on a permanent home.

Its diet consists of small rodents, eggs of ground nesting birds, cactus fruit and whatever insects it may capture. Fresh diggings around the bases of cacti and shrubs often indicate that this animal has been searching for grubs and beetles that eat these plants' roots. These skunks add a thick layer of fat in the fall, but they do not hibernate.

The powerful, nauseating scent released by skunks when danger threatens is secreted by two glands near the base of the tail. The skunk contracts the muscles around these glands, spraying the secretion several feet. If possible, the tail is held up out of the way while the scent is being discharged. After spraying, skunks wallow in moist earth to clean their fur.

RANGE: Southwestern United States and northern Mexico.

HABITAT: Lower and Upper Sonoran zones, occasionally in the Transition Zone. Any locality with sufficient ground cover.

HOGNOSE SKUNK
Conepatus mesoleucus

DESCRIPTION: A slow, awkward nocturnal animal with a long nose, lusterless, rusty-black sides, white back and tail. Total length about 26 inches (65 centimeters), tail 12 inches (30 centimeters) long. Body color is brownish-black with a broad white stripe covering the back. The tail is all white and a white stripe down the face may be present. The fur is short, sparse and coarse. The long, flexible nose is naked and has a piglike termination. Front and hind feet are armed with long claws. From two to four young are born in early summer.

The hognose skunk is a rooter, a slow rather powerful animal that plows through the leaf mold and soft loam in search of food. The long nose with its piglike snout and the long claws are well adapted for uncovering the grubs and worms that this skunk eats. The coarse, sparse coat lacks the gleaming highlights of other skunks' coats. The tail, though lacking in luster, is white and bushy. The small eyes are dull and expressionless.

These skunks appear to pursue their life's activities with indifference to their surroundings. At night they rustle noisily through the dry leaves. However, this species is equipped with the same adaptations as others of its family. As it buries its nose in a bed of leaf mold, its rear is protected with a chemical-emitting gland capable of repelling any natural enemy. Although a carnivore, it rarely catches small rodents or birds because of its slow movements. Instead, it must glean the remainder of kills of other predators or eat whatever food it comes across.

Since the bulk of its diet is insects, the hognose skunk is usually found around soft, loamy soil where beetles and worms can be unearthed and near deep beds of leaf mold where grubs are found. In desert country such areas are found almost entirely in deeper canyons. Although the hognose skunk's range encompasses most of the country for 200 miles (322 kilometers) on both sides of the Mexican border from Texas to California, it is not abundant anywhere.

Its threats are the encroachments of civilization on its habitat. If banished from its rooting grounds, it may not be able to adapt to a new, unfamiliar habitat.

RANGE: Southwestern Texas, southern New Mexico, southern Arizona, northwestern Mexico.

HABITAT: Upper and Lower Sonoran zones. Washes and canyons in the low desert valleys.

SPOTTED SKUNK
Spilogale gracilis

DESCRIPTION: A small, nocturnal, black and white animal, noticeably heavier behind with the terminal half of its bushy tail white. Total length is about 16 inches (40 centimeters), tail about 6 inches (15 centimeters). Body color black with various white spots on the face, four narrow white stripes along front half of the back, the rump variously blotched with white, tail half black and half white. Ears small and round. Young, from three to six, born in early summer.

The common name, civet cat, applied to this animal is a misnomer. Civet cats are an Old World animal not native to any part of the United States. In many parts of the Southwest these skunks are commonly known as "hydrophobia" skunks or "phoby" cats. The origin of these names is difficult to determine since these creatures are no more subject to this disease than any other animal. In many places this unfortunate connotation has led to their indiscriminate slaughter.

Any person who travels the Southwest deserts will eventually meet this smallest member of the skunk family. Knowledge of their habits is a worthwhile endeavor. Whether the introduction can be called a social success will depend almost entirely on the human element involved. Human reactions vary, but skunks will dependably react one of two ways: either they will or they will not spray.

To avoid the strained relations that invariably develop should the skunk decide that defensive measures are necessary, a few tips are suggested: don't attempt to pick up *Spilogale* by its tail. Stories that claim it is defenseless in this position are false. Don't approach too closely if the skunk seems nervous. By all means, retreat if it begins to stamp its front feet. This is a danger signal that warns, "You've come close enough." Don't presume too much on short acquaintance. While skunks quickly become tame, they are still wild creatures that must consider humans as enemies. Any quick startling movement or sound may cause them to resort to tactics distressing to all concerned.

RANGE: California, Arizona, New Mexico, northwestern Mexico.

HABITAT: Lower Sonoran, Upper Sonoran and Transition zones. Rocky areas from cactus desert to pines.

PORCUPINE
Erethizoŋ dorsatum

DESCRIPTION: The only mammal native to the United States that bears quills. Total length about 30 inches (75 centimeters), tail about 9 inches (22.5 centimeters). General color salt-and-pepper, tending to be dark. The guard hairs may be 6 inches (15 centimeters) or more long, the under fur 2 or 5 inches (5 or 12 centimeters) long. Mingled among this coat are thousands of quills ranging from an inch (2.5 centimeters) in length on the tail to as much as 4 inches (10 centimeters) on the back. Ears small, lying close to the head. Eyes small and dull. The chisel-like front teeth are long, broad, and yellow. The front feet are armed with long, curved claws; claws of hind feet are shorter.

It may be surprising that the porcupine—associated with the coniferous forests of the north—is also found commonly in the pinyon-juniper association of the Upper Sonoran Zone and uncommonly in the vast stretches of the lower desert. Because the porcupine is thought to have come from South America after the last Ice Age, it is probable that the northern animals simply extended their range. They are all the same species, with slight differences due to environmental conditions. Although it survives well in the arid country, its numbers are fewer than those in the north. In the Upper Sonoran Zone the inner bark of pine and juniper furnish only a part of the diet. At lower altitudes devoid of conifers this porcupine eats mesquite beans and grass, browses on low shrubs such as Mormon tea and jojoba, and occasionally may strip some bark from the mesquite and ironwood trees. Perhaps this desert growth supplies some of the necessary minerals lacking in the northern porcupine's diet which includes axe handles, harness and the tops of kitchen tables for the salt they contain.

The adaptation for which this animal is most notorious is its quills, actually modified hairs. They range in size from tiny needles an inch (2.5 centimeters) long and as thin as fine pencil lead to 4 inches (10 centimeters) long and as thick as a wooden matchstick. All the quills are white with black tips and are needle sharp, having innumerable barbs near the points which prevent their being easily removed. The shortest quills are on the tail, the longest on the back and shoulders. The underside of the animal is unprotected.

This flaw in its almost perfect defense leads the porcupine to strenuously resist any attempt to overturn it. Its favorite defensive posture is a crouch with the head between the front legs. In this position it endeavors to keep its back towards the enemy. The slightest touch on this part of its anatomy provokes a flailing retaliation with the muscular tail. Dozens of quills can be driven into the enemy's flesh. Often the target is the face of the predator. Contrary to popular notions, porcupines do not "throw" their quills any distance. The quills, held by their barbed points, eventually work deeper and finally may kill the victim. Mountain lions, fishers, coyotes and bears are foremost among the few predators which attack porcupines. Mountain lions, most expert, can flip porcupines on their backs to kill and eat them. However, even they

receive a few quills in the face and forelegs.

Dogs are especially prone to attack porcupines with the usual disastrous results. Extracting the quills is a painful process. One method this writer suggests is to catch the dog, draw his forelegs back along the body and wrap the dog tightly in a blanket, leaving only the head exposed. Cut off about 1/8 inch (3.18 millimeters) from the butt end of the quills with scissors. This partially collapses the hollow quills and makes extraction less difficult. With pliers, pull each one out with a sharp jerk, staying clear of the dog's snapping jaws. This treatment is advised only if a veterinarian cannot be reached.

The porcupine resembles an awkward, nearsighted bear in many of its actions. Typical gait is a slow, deliberate waddle interrupted by pauses to sniff and perhaps nibble a plant along the trail. When feeding on the ground, it bears its weight mainly on the hind feet, while the forefeet are used to gather stalks. Because of its poor sight most of its food is selected by taste or smell. If browsing a branch, it will stand erect on its hind feet, using the tail as a prop, and try to pull the tip within reach of its teeth. When aloft it uses the same tactics, with its curved claws helping to hold it to the bark. The porcupine, not a dainty eater, smacks its lips like a pig and drinks like a horse, thrusting its mouth beneath the surface of the water and drawing in gulps.

Due to their relative immunity to injury or death from predators, porcupines live long lives. Average lifespan is uncertain but porcupines have been found that are old enough to be blind and have stiff joints.

Although they divide their time between trees and the ground, porcupines have semi-permanent dens usually located in the rocks along a ridge. Here one young is born in the spring, averaging a pound (.45 kilograms) in weight. The incisors and sometimes a few molars are already through the gums. The quills are soft and harmless but within a few hours harden enough to be dangerous to any enemy. The fur is black. The long yellow guard hairs do not develop until some months later.

This independent youngster almost immediately begins to eat tender grass and herbs, so the weaning period can be said to start at birth. At two months, it is usually entirely weaned and finding its own food. For the first year it keeps to the ground, or may climb a tree only a short distance. It is more vocal than the parents and will complain in a high, thin voice if disturbed.

RANGE: Most of New Mexico, west Texas, Utah and Colorado, eastern half of Arizona and south into Mexico.

HABITAT: Principally in the Upper Sonoran Zone, but also occasionally seen in the Lower Sonoran Zone. Among pinyon and juniper, but also along washes in Lower Sonoran.

BLACKTAIL JACKRABBIT
Lepus californicus

DESCRIPTION: A large jackrabbit with black-tipped ears. Average total length about 24 inches (60 centimeters), tail 3.5 inches (8.75 centimeters). General color a pale gray, darker along the back and lighter underneath. Ears up to 6 inches (15 centimeters) long, almost naked inside, with sparse fur on the outer surfaces and black tips. Top of tail black, undersurface white. Eyes prominent, a clear yellowish brown. Young, three to six, several litters a year.

Commonly known throughout the West, these jackrabbits are technically not rabbits but hares. Rabbits are born naked and blind, while hares have short thick fur coats and well-developed sight when born. This basic distinction established, for purposes of discussion it will here be called blacktail jackrabbit because of the familiarity of that common name.

Jackrabbits are born in a nest, usually hollowed out in a clump of grass. When very small they have a dark stripe down the forehead, rather short ears and a tawny gray coat. As they mature, the ears grow out of all proportion to the rest of the animal, and new clear gray hair replaces the tawny coat. Within a few weeks they are able to leave the nest for short ventures and from this point their progress is rapid. Soon they are foraging for themselves, and their mother is likely preparing a nest for a new litter.

In the bitter race for survival forced on Southwest wildlife, jackrabbits are holding their own. The jackrabbits are among the most prolific mammals. In the absence of predators to check this increase, they would multiply so rapidly that their food supplies would become scarce. A disease known as tularemia also controls their population without cutting too deeply into their numbers. Instead, those weak, old and sick individuals who would be destroyed by natural enemies are among those that suffer mortality.

Their physical construction makes their capture difficult. Mounted in the sides of its long narrow skull the jackrabbit's slightly protuberant eyes have a horizontal range of a full circle. With a slight head movement, the rabbit can cover the entire field. Vertical coverage is nearly as comprehensive.

At night the huge ears take up the constant vigil. They have coverage corresponding to the eyes, and can be rotated to cover the entire field.

Unlike its larger cousin, the antelope jackrabbit, the blacktail does not often "freeze" and depend on its protective coloration to foil discovery. If startled by a person, the rabbit often uses a slow and erratic gait, with a few slow leaps alternating with faster bounds. But the rush of an animal predator is met with a series of short sprinting leaps that change to graceful, soaring bounds as racing speed is attained. This speed cannot be matched by any native animal predator in the Southwest.

To these desert-wise creatures water is more a luxury than a necessity. Although they do not disdain it if available, they will not go any great distance to obtain it. Curiously, among the smaller animals, the jackrabbits can more easily travel to the infrequent watering places than can ground squirrels or small rodents which must stay closer to their homes. Instead, jacks depend on their food to provide sufficient moisture. To exist on this limited amount of water, the jackrabbit must conform to certain behavior and confine its diet to the most succulent foods seasonally available.

The blacktail jackrabbit is most active during the later afternoon and night, when humidity is relatively high and temperature low. Consequently, the least moisture will be given up through respiration and perspiration. By early morning the animal has eaten its fill and prepares to retire for the day.

With no burrow to retire to, the jackrabbit needs more succulent foods than ground squirrels or the woodrat. These it obtains from fresh green grass available in quantities after summer and winter rains. Between these periods of high living come the two dry seasons, spring and fall. During these times the animal subsists on leaves from low-hanging mesquite branches and joints from the prickly pear. The tender mesquite leaves are especially relished since they come out when the short-lived winter grass has withered. Although eaten all year, the heaviest consumption of prickly pear is in the fall when little succulent food can be found.

With the conversion of much of its range to agriculture, the jackrabbit has found other than native foods to satisfy its needs. In recent years chili peppers have been grown in valleys in southeastern Arizona. After the bright red pods are harvested, they are laid out to dry on the long runways of abandoned air strips. The flesh of these peppers is succulent and sweet, but the seeds are fiery hot. The jackrabbits in the area come at night and eat the fruits. At each spot where a pod has been taken, a small pile of seeds lies discarded, showing the jackrabbits' discerning tastes.

RANGE: All of the southwestern United States from central Texas to the Pacific Ocean and from Colorado, Utah, Idaho and Oregon to the Mexican border. Common in the deserts of northern Mexico.

HABITAT: Upper and Lower Sonoran zones. Any terrain which can support enough plant life to feed them.

ANTELOPE JACKRABBIT
Lepus alleni

DESCRIPTION: A large hare with buffy-white sides and a conspicuous white rump patch which it "aims" as it lopes away. Total length about 26 inches (65 centimeters), tail 3.5 inches (8.75 centimeters). Body white to buffy white, darker on back. Tail white underneath, black above. Ears white. Of special interest is the large rump patch of long white hair which can be moved from one flank to the other. Young usually four, or up to six, born in early summer. Although slightly larger than the blacktail species, the antelope jackrabbit seems much larger, possibly because of its longer fur and light coloration. It also possesses certain other peculiarities that set it apart from the blacktail. The white rump patch, from which it gets its name, is one of them. When the animal is undisturbed, the dark hair over this part of the back covers the white portion so that it is unnoticeable against a background of dry grass and adobe soil. When a startled rabbit flees, the long, white erectile hair stands up around this darker area, concealing it so the rear of the animal appears fluffy white.

The purpose of flaunting this eye-catching flag is not precisely known. It is certainly a deliberate attempt to attract attention. When a big desert jack is startled from its resting place, it will run diagonally away from its pursuer for perhaps a hundred feet (30 meters), with its rump patch thrown over on the hip closest to its enemy. The rabbit will suddenly change course, cutting diagonally in the opposite direction. The rump patch is shifted to other hip, again to face the pursuer. This could confuse the predator and give the rabbit extra time to escape. It is unlikely that the flag warns other rabbits, for the low growth typical of their habitat would prevent the patch from being seen at any distance.

The antelope jackrabbit is a member of a group known as the white-sided jackrabbits. They inhabit central and northern Mexico, except for this species which is also native to Arizona. Another is said to be present in limited numbers in southern New Mexico.

It lives in the most arid parts of Arizona, among the valleys and hills covered with drought-resistant shrubs and trees typical of the Lower Sonoran Zone. Under and around these shrubs and trees grow the grasses, herbs and cacti that this large hare eats. Desert grasses cure into excellent hay which retains much of the food value of the living plants. During fall and winter the antelope jack eats much of this dry food, adding moisture to its diet by foraging on cactus pads. Generally, its food requirements are the same as the blacktail's, whose range it partially shares.

Life histories of the two are also similar. Young are born in a well-concealed nest, usually above ground, and at birth are fully furred. Normally one litter is produced each year. Both species are nocturnal. Days are spent crouched in a shallow basin under the sparse shade of a shrub or small tree. Able to outrun any pursuer, the rabbit will usually attempt to evade detection rather than leave its resting place. Its methods are interesting: normally it will sit quietly with ears erect. When it hears something approaching, it becomes excited. The ears are turned towards the intruder, and the animal may stand erect on its long hind legs to get a better view. As the intruder approaches more closely, the rabbit will sink slowly to the ground, ears still picking up every sound. When the disturber is at very close range, the rabbit lays its ears slowly back along the shoulders and freezes in position. It will remain there until driven from the resting place, or until the enemy leaves. If the rabbit decides to run, it will raise its ears and in a second take flight.

With perfect coordination the animal gracefully soars through the air in a series of arcs, sinking to ground only to leave in undulating bounds covering 10 to 15 feet (3 to 4.5 meters). If an enemy is in hot pursuit, they are long low leaps, skimming the ground. If unhurried, they are short jumps that offer a chance to look around in mid-air. On high speed runs a rocking motion is evident as the hare touches ground. Inspection of the tracks shows that the front feet are pushed sharply against the earth at the termination of the leap. This shoves the front quarters up away from the ground; about 2 yards (1.8 meters) further the hind feet come down with the full body weight on them. With a sharp kick of the spring-steel legs, the rabbit is in the air again on the next bound. An amusing variation is a series of jumps made with only the hind feet touching the ground and the body erect, enabling the rabbit to pick up speed quickly.

Normally the animal does not seem hurried—even during a chase it seems to float indolently, content merely to maintain its lead. Predators are almost always frustrated in their attempts to capture these rabbits. Only coyotes continue pursuit, succeeding occasionally in catching a young or old rabbit.

Despite their impressive flight ability, these jackrabbits, never common animals, appear to be having their numbers reduced by inroads of civilization.

RANGE: Southern Arizona and northwestern Mexico.

HABITAT: Lower Sonoran Zone. Desert valleys and grasslands.

DESERT COTTONTAIL
Sylvilagus audubonii

DESCRIPTION: Cottontail rabbits are similar throughout the United States. Total length of western forms averages about 15 inches (37.5 centimeters), of which the tail accounts for about 1 inch (2.5 centimeters). Color buffy gray on back and sides, with darker shading on shoulders and legs. Ears relatively long for a mammal of this size, ranging from a little over 2 to almost 3 inches (5 to 7.5 centimeters), measured from the notch. Eyes large, whiskers above the mouth. Front legs short, hind legs also short with hind feet 3 to 4 inches (7.5 to 10 centimeters) long. The "powder puff" tail is dark gray above and pure white below. Young, two to six, with several litters born each year.

This species, with several subspecies, inhabits all the southwestern states in such numbers that it cannot easily be overlooked. Its habits are similar to its eastern relatives, modified to some extent by the sterner conditions under which it lives. Perhaps no mammal of comparable size has so many natural enemies. Although the death rate must be high from these predators' inroads, cottontail numbers do not appear to be declining. In fact, it often becomes so numerous that its numbers are reduced by disease. Natural enemies that control them include every carnivore of half their size or more that inhabits their range. Among these are snakes and large predatory birds, both diurnal and nocturnal. If these predators were eliminated, it is possible that the cottontails would increase until food would be the central limiting factor.

In the Midwest these rabbits live in brushy places, venturing onto the grasslands mainly for food and to raise their families. The nests are cleverly concealed in hollows lined with soft grass. The mothers do not remain in the immediate vicinity, apparently seeking shelter of the brush during the day and returning to feed the young at night. On the desert a nest is seldom found above ground. Usually they are deep in a burrow, perhaps one appropriated from a large rodent or remodeled from the old workings of a badger. In this burrow, insulated from the heat and safe from many predators, the females bear several litters of young each year. Newborn rabbits are blind and almost naked, comparatively helpless until their eyes open. Their progress is then so rapid that they are able to leave the nest when small.

Although fast on their feet, cottontails do not rely entirely on their speed to avoid capture. Instead, they resort to a zigzag dash for the nearest burrow or clump of brush in which to hide.

RANGE: All the southwestern states.

HABITAT: Upper and Lower Sonoran zones. Not restricted to any type of terrain; in general found wherever sufficient cover is available.

WHITE-THROATED WOODRAT
Neotoma albigula

DESCRIPTION: A rodent somewhat resembling a house rat except for its prominent ears. The specific name *albigula* means white throat. Adults are up to 13 inches (32.5 centimeters) in total length; tail lightly furred, about 6 inches (15 centimeters) long. Upper parts are light brown, lower parts white or sometimes buffy, throat pure white even to the bases of the hairs. The ears are exceptionally large, lending a rabbit look to the face; eyes large and dark brown. These features, together with the long, silky whiskers, give the woodrat a rather appealing appearance. The two to four young are born during the spring and by fall are able to be on their own.

This pack rat of the south shares the inclination of the northern trade rat in carrying away any shiny or metallic object it fancies. In the place of the article it may leave some worthless piece of barter. Although this is probably merely coincidence, it occurs often enough to have given the animal the names "trade" or "pack" rat. When its petty larceny extends to the valuables in people's homes or camps, the habit can become somewhat less than amusing.

The woodrat's home soon becomes familiar to even the casual observer. The mound over the nest is built of numerous items, but the shape of the pile always looks like a pile of rubbish. Even when a dwelling is chosen in a cliff crevice, a pile of sticks and clods of dirt around the entrance is inevitable for defense against predators.

The nest is a marvel of construction, with thick warm walls woven of shredded bark or coarse grass, lined with softer fibers. It usually rests directly on the ground or in a shallow excavation, covered with the protective mound.

One woodrat home was found in and around a large prickly pear cactus in a wide sandy wash bordered by the blue paloverde. It contained a number of dry paloverde sticks, the largest ¾ inches (19.05 millimeters) in diameter and 24 inches (60 centimeters) long; cow chips, tin cans, joints of cane cactus, jumping cactus and prickly pear, pieces of newspaper and a fruit jar lid. Many detached spine clusters appeared to have been brought in singly. The mound was 4.5 feet (13.5 centimeters) wide and 27 inches (67.5 centimeters) high. The largest stick weighed 7-9/16 ounces (.21 kilograms), considerably more than the weight of an average woodrat.

The woodrat's food depends on seasonal availability. During the cooler part of the year it eats mesquite beans, seeds of various grasses and shrubs, and the bark of the smaller branches of mesquite and paloverde trees. It has been known to girdle the resinous branches of the ocotillo.

As the summer heat approaches, the woodrat has no cool underground burrow in which to take refuge. The porous nest and mound become tinder-dry and hot under the sun. With the loss of body moisture that occurs, the woodrat turns to more succulent food, usually the commonly available prickly pear *(Opuntia engelmanii)*. Tender young pads growing with the benefit of the previous winter's rains are the first to be attacked.

To maintain its moisture balance during hot summer days, the woodrat rests quietly in the coolest part of the mound during the day and indulges in only limited movement during the times of highest humidity and coolest temperatures (at night).

Among its predators are foxes, coyotes, bobcats and snakes. In addition it is a host of the blood-sucking kissing bug *(Triatoma* sp.) the notorious "walpai tiger" of the Southwest. The insect is most active during May and June but its numbers diminish after the summer rains begin.

This native rodent is not to be confused with the common domestic rats *(Rattus* sp.) which are European importations. The woodrat is a scrupulously clean animal whose adaptations to desert living still hold a great deal of knowledge for people.

RANGE: Woodrats may be found throughout the United States. The white-throated woodrat inhabits Arizona, New Mexico, and northern Mexico.

HABITAT: Upper and Lower Sonoran zones. Nests may be found in almost any kind of terrain covered by a conspicuous mound of sticks, bark, stones and cactus joints.

VALLEY POCKET GOPHER
Thomomys bottae

DESCRIPTION: This pocket gopher is more likely to be recognized by its home than physical appearance. It is heavy-set, about 11 inches (27.5 centimeters) long, tail about 3 inches (7.5 centimeters). General color a dark brown. Ears and eyes small. Legs short, feet armed with stout claws, especially on the front feet. Terminal quarter of tail usually bare. Young, three to six, one litter a season. Because of its great elevational distribution, several varieties of this species are found. In the desert many animals are nocturnal, or if they are active in the day they retire to burrows part of the time. Only a few spend most of their time in total darkness. The pocket gopher shares this distinction only with the bats and shrews. The pocket gopher alone can be said to live in the velvety blackness of an underground tunnel all its life with a rare glimpse of daylight only when it hastily throws out a load of dirt or ventures a few feet from its burrow to gather some herbage.

This busy miner digs its food. As it tunnels, it finds roots, tubers, bulbs and corms which it attacks with its chisel-like teeth. In larger plants like the century plants and sotols, it may eat into the large fleshy bases and seriously damage the plant. On smaller plants the gophers not only eat the root system but pull the whole stem and foliage into its tunnel where it can be eaten leisurely. Like most rodents, the pocket gopher will store food when it finds a surplus. Though these stores of roots and bulbs are rather perishable, as much as a gallon of this material has been found in one burrow.

This gopher does not take on a layer of fat and hibernate like many other rodents that live in the ground. Instead, it remains active year-round in an unremitting search for food. In the desert, plants with tuberous roots are usually not difficult to locate throughout the year.

Although rarely seen itself, the labor of this animal is much in evidence. The characteristic mounds have no definite shape or size but are evidently thrown up with one purpose—to get rid of as much waste material as possible in as little time as it can. The mounds are usually close to a group of underground chambers. A typical burrow might include a nursery fitted with a soft nest, a living room and a toilet room. The latter is a necessity in such confined quarters. When this room has been filled, it is sealed off from the tunnel and a new one is excavated.

As usual with animals that lead a specialized existence, the gopher has adapted to live quite comfortably within the narrow limits of its environment. Adaptations include the long digging claws of the front feet, the cylinder-shaped body with its short legs and the heavy fur coat. Perhaps the most remarkable adaptation is the bare tip of the short tail—a sensory organ that feels the way when the gopher backs out of a tunnel too narrow to turn around in. Although the main runways that connect the living quarters and various other chambers are roomy, the tunnels are dug narrowly to avoid removing more material than necessary. The pocket gopher can move backward almost as fast as it can go forward. With the development of these adaptations to an underground life, other senses have deteriorated. The eyes have become small and shortsighted, and the ears are small. Nevertheless, gophers can quickly sight an enemy at close range and can detect the vibrations of footsteps from some distance.

The pockets that give this gopher its common name are principally a means of carrying food, not excavated earth. Tunneling is accomplished by packing the loose dirt between the forelegs and throat, then thrusting with hind legs to the entrance of the tunnel. On one of its infrequent short trips above ground, the gopher hastily collects a load of greens, re-enters the tunnel and plugs the entrance with several more loads of dirt. During the outside excursions the gopher is most vulnerable in the face of the superior speed and agility of its enemies—bobcats, foxes, coyotes and hawks.

RANGE: Southwestern United States and northern Mexico.

HABITAT: Almost all life zones from the Lower Sonoran to the Canadian. Loose soil and abundant plant life, found usually around springs or marshy spots called *cienegas* in Spanish.

CACTUS MOUSE
Peromyscus spp.

DESCRIPTION: Cactus mice are about the size of an ordinary house mouse but have large ears, haired tails and usually white feet. Because of the similarities of the several species and their wide range, identification can best be accomplished through a few outstanding characteristics. These are small rodents, the average individual measuring about 7 to 8 inches (17.5 to 20 centimeters) in total length, the tail about 3 or 4 inches (7.65 or 10 centimeters). Most species are buffy gray above, shading to a brighter buff along the sides and white underneath. The color of the feet explains another common name, white-footed mouse. The ears are large for the animal's size, sparsely covered with a sprinkling of short, fine hairs, or, in some species, naked. The eyes are prominent and appear black, although in a bright light they have a brownish tinge. Long silky whiskers give the face a woodrat appearance. The tail is sparsely furred with brown hairs above and white below. Young, four to six, born at any time of the year.

Deer mice are gentle, strictly nocturnal and seldom seen unless their nests or hideouts are accidentally discovered. They live anywhere: rock crevices, hollow trees, and flotsam remaining from desert flash floods. All are acceptable nesting sites. They unhesitatingly move into old barns and sheds or houses. Their nests are carefully constructed, the outer walls of coarse fibers and the interior lined with the softest materials available. They are active year-round.

Food consists mainly of any seeds, nuts and small berries they can find. They spend a good deal of time gathering desert grass seeds. They are also adept climbers and will climb trees and shrubs for any acceptable food. In such exposed locations many are caught by owls. On the ground they are prey for all nocturnal predators from shrews to bears. Their high reproduction rate allows the animals to survive attacks on their numbers.

RANGE: Cactus Mouse: in southern New Mexico, west and southwest Arizona, west Texas and Mexico. Deer Mouse: widely distributed in all the southwestern states.

HABITAT: All the life zones of the Southwest. Depending on the species, can be found in almost any association; quickly adapt to dwellings.

73

POCKET MOUSE
Perognathus spp.

DESCRIPTION: As with *Peromyscus,* the similarities of the group make it possible to give general characteristics. Pocket mice are closely related to the kangaroo rat. They live in burrows in the ground, have cheek pouches in which to carry food, and have rather long hind legs and shorter forelegs. The largest, the intermediate pocket mouse, is about 7 inches (17.5 centimeters) long with a tail about 4 inches (10 centimeters) long. Baird's pocket mouse, is considered the smallest rodent in the Southwest, only a little more than 4 inches (10 centimeters) long, with a tail half that length. Most species are distinctly yellowish or buffy above, shading to the usual lighter or white bellies and feet. The ears are small. In many species the tail is nearly as long as the body and in a few species is slighty longer. Young from three to six, with two litters a season.

These are definitely desert mice. They inhabit rocky and mellow soils, and they burrow in the open away from overhanging shrubs. The dirt is cast to one side of the burrow and since passageways are small and shallow, conspicuous mounds are not formed. When retiring for the day, these strictly nocturnal mice commonly plug the entrances to their burrows with earth to defend against enemies and keep up the humidity within the underground chambers.

Pocket mice and kangaroo rats share many adaptations to desert life. Restricted to the ground because of their poor climbing ability, pocket mice subsist almost entirely on grass and weed seeds. They live well on this dry food and are able to endure months without free water. Evidently they, too, are able to manufacture their own water during digestion. They have the same enemies, although pocket mice are more vulnerable because they lack the bounding, erratic flight of the bannertail. Their burrows are shallow and most predators, including badgers, foxes and coyotes, are able to dig them out.

RANGE: Throughout the Southwest.

HABITAT: Upper and Lower Sonoran zones. Mesas and open valleys. Burrows will be found in drier locations.

GRASSHOPPER MOUSE
Onychomys spp.

DESCRIPTION: A medium-sized mouse with a short tail. Coloring is buffy above and lighter to white underneath. Feet, undersurfaces, and tip of tail white. Ears small. Feet are round rather than long as in most mice. The tail is noticeably short in most species, the one outstanding exception in the Southwest being the southern grasshopper mouse, *O. torridus,* a resident of the Lower Sonoran Zone. Average total length about 6 inches (15 centimeters), tail about 2 inches (5 centimeters). Young, four to six, usually two litters a year.

These short-tailed mice are perhaps the most interesting of the mouse family. All mice can be insectivorous and carnivorous to some degree, because all vary their diets of grain and seeds with some insect or bit of meat that may come their way. But because insects make up such a large part of its diet, it might seem proper to call the grasshopper mouse an insectivore by choice. It also avidly searches for flesh of warm blooded animals, but because it is not physically equipped to capture them, it must eat those killed by some other agent.

The grasshopper mouse is a nomad among its kind, lacking a permanent nest and well established territory from which it harvests food. Its wanderings are irregular, and it depends on old, abandoned burrows of other animals for refuge. Rodents up to twice its size cannot resist its advances to take over their nests.

This animal's common name, ''calling mouse,'' comes from a smooth, long high-pitched note heard for some distance that it uses perhaps to locate other grasshopper mice. The sound is entirely unlike the sharp, short squeaks other mice use. It may also warn other individuals to stay away from a given territory.
RANGE: All of the southwestern states.
HABITAT: Mainly in the Upper Sonoran Zone. Usually on open mesas, grassy or with scattered trees.

BANNERTAIL KANGAROO RAT
Dipodomys spectabilis

DESCRIPTION: A fawn-colored rodent with a long tail tipped with a white brush. The bounding gait is distinctive. The adult is about 14 inches (35 centimeters) in total length; the body is short and compact; the tail is long and slender with a prominent white brush at the tip. The hind legs are long and powerful, front legs short, usually held out of sight under the throat. The eyes are large, appear black, are set back on the sides of the head. Color above a general dark buff, with lighter areas around eyes and back of ears. Underparts white. An average of three young are born in late spring (May and June). *D. spectabilis* is one of the largest of several species of this genus.

These rats are commonly seen at night in the glare of headlights as they bounce across the road, propelled by their long hind legs and guided by their long tail. Although their diet consists mainly of air-dried seeds, they can exist for months without free water because of a complex chemical process which creates water from the digestion of dry food. In addition to creating moisture, they conserve it several ways. The kangaroo rat does not perspire. It also plugs the entrances to its burrow with dirt during the day, sealing out heat and retaining humidity. This remarkable animal has modified its habits so extensively that it actively shuns water or succulent foods most of the time. Green food may be eaten sparingly at certain times, a dewdrop licked from a drooping stem, or some flavorful bulb dug and eaten. However, these are the exceptions and are not necessary to the well-being of this rodent.

It has a violent aversion to water or moisture on the fur and stays in its burrow during wet weather. To clean itself it resorts to sand baths. From an oily gland on its upper back the kangaroo rat dresses its fur, somewhat as a duck uses oil to dress its feathers and make them waterproof and buoyant. Excess oil on the fur makes it matted and sticky. Wallowing in dry sand removes this oil and keeps the fur shiny and fluffy. The strange patterns left in these soft wallows puzzled scientists for a time. They are merely splashes in the rat's sandy swimming hole.

Among themselves these rodents are extremely unsociable. If confined together, fights break out which usually end in the death of one of the combatants. Principal weapons are the long hind claws with which they rake and tear their opponent. In the wild, one individual occupies a mound except when the female is raising young. During this period the male is banished from the family. By fall the young have matured and are able to make their own burrow and gather food for the winter.

The short front legs are employed in gathering the heads of seeds from various grasses and stuffing them into the capacious cheek pouches and then into the storage rooms underground. These storerooms are jealously guarded and may explain why the adults do not socialize. It is certainly the reason *D. spectabilis* has an active enmity against *D. merriami,* a smaller species that raids its food stores. Much of the bannertail's food is processed at the burrow, evidenced by the loose husks found

around the burrow entrances.

Among the bannertail's natural enemies are coyotes, foxes, badgers, owls and snakes. Its only defense consists of its bounding, erratic flight and the many burrow entrances into which it may flee. This large species is capable of jumping 10 or more feet (3 meters). By swinging the long rudder-like tail to one side it can change course abruptly, a maneuver designed to confuse pursuers. In the burrow it is reasonably safe from all but snakes. These take a heavy toll on the kangaroo rat population, several species subsisting almost entirely on this rodent.

These rats seldom utter any vocal sounds, but, as with most rodents, they can communicate by thumping the ground with their hind feet. Exactly what is communicated is uncertain. A light slap on the surface of the mound will sometimes bring an answering thump if the burrow is occupied. This sound carries well and can be heard from several feet away on a quiet day.

RANGE: Southeastern Arizona, west Texas and southern New Mexico.

HABITAT: Upper part of the Lower Sonoran Zone. A burrow with many entrances under a mound of excavated earth, often located among the roots of a desert shrub.

CLIFF CHIPMUNK
Eutamias dorsalis

DESCRIPTION: A large chipmunk with faint stripes, white ears, and gray neck and back. Total length about 9.5 inches (23.75 centimeters), tail 4.5 inches (11.25 centimeters). The stripes characteristic of the chipmunk are most easily seen in the thin summer coat. The heavy gray winter coat obscures all but the black stripe down the middle of the back. Tail broad and bushy for a chipmunk, gray above and striped below with rufous, black, buff, and gray. Ears white outside with rufous edge. Sides of legs yellowish brown. Young, four to six, with often two litters in a season, the first being born early in the spring.

This is the only chipmunk that can be said to live in the southwest deserts. A close relative *(E. merriami merodionalis)*, the peninsula chipmunk, inhabits the Lower Sonoran Zone in lower California. Various other chipmunks native to the Southwest may descend to the edge of the Upper Sonoran Zone at times, but the cliff chipmunk is the only representative of *Eutamias* that is a permanent resident of the Upper Sonoran Zone. Its presence there is so unexpected that it often goes unnoticed, mistaken for the Harris' Antelope squirrel, whose range it overlaps.

The most noticeable difference between this species and the Harris' Antelope squirrel is its tail. The cliff chipmunk's tail is longer and bushier than the Harris' squirrel's, and it is more obviously displayed. When alarmed or curious, this chipmunk will wave its tail slowly and sinuously, seldom with the excited, jerky motion of the ground squirrels in the same situation. The coloration of the two species is quite different too, the Harris' Antelope squirrel being a darker gray and lacking the rich buff around the tail and legs.

Normally thought of as a forest dweller, the cliff chipmunk has become well adapted to a dry environment. They build their nests in deep cliff crevices or under a mass of talus, using dried grass stems and soft material. One or more storage chambers are also prepared to hold food.

During the dryness of late spring and early fall the chipmunk exists by obtaining moisture from cactus fruits and berries or succulent roots and bulbs. The diet consists principally of dry grass seeds, acorns, juniper berries and pinyon nuts. It is doubtful if this chipmunk ever hibernates. During bad weather it is probably snug in its nest eating food gathered during warmer weather.

The cliff chipmunk is wonderfully agile and active. It nonchalantly scampers up precipitous canyon walls and overhangs. Should it fall, the bushy tail is sent in a whirling motion to slow the speed of the descent.

RANGE: New Mexico and the eastern half of Arizona. Throughout most of Utah and extending into Nevada.

HABITAT: The Upper Sonoran Zone. Rocky canyons with oak, juniper or pinyon along the rims.

Harris' Antelope Squirrel
Ammospermophilus harrisii

DESCRIPTION: A small ground squirrel with a white stripe along each side. Total length about 9 inches (22.5 centimeters), tail about 3 inches (7.5 centimeters). Upper parts gray, with a white line around the eye. Feet and underparts lighter gray. The bushy tail is dark gray above and lighter below. Ears small. A conspicuous white stripe extends along the sides from shoulder to flank.

Harris' Antelope squirrels live in the desert foothills. Their burrows are usually excavated among the rocks and are so difficult to dig out that most predators pass them by. Snakes are their chief enemy below ground. From the air red-tailed hawks often catch an individual that has ventured too far afield. When pursued, these speedy squirrels often seek safety in the shelter of a clump of bushes rather than following the usual procedure of popping into the nearest hole. Commonly associated with the prickly pear, they seldom resort to any part of it except the fruits for food. Even during drought the pads are seldom, if ever, eaten. This reluctance to eat the pads of such a succulent plant denies them a source of moisture used by most other rodents.

Due to the confiding nature of these sprightly squirrels, they are seen at close range more often than the timid roundtails which inhabit the same range. Excellent climbers, they will often make their presence known by a long, shrill trill that resembles a bird's in clarity. The approach of any real or imagined danger is greeted by violent flicks of the expressive tail and vocal expressions of disapproval. Harris' Antelope squirrels can be annoying to bird photographers in southern Arizona deserts. They quickly take charge of feeding stations and carry food to their burrows. Efforts to frighten these striped marauders only result in scaring away the birds. Only when they attempt to intimidate the thrashers and Gila woodpeckers do they meet their match. These aggressive birds pounce on the squirrels, followed by the squirrels' hasty departure, sometimes, with the loss of a few tufts of hair. However, the writer has seen several encounters in which both hair and feathers flew, the ground squirrel emerging victorious.

Like other squirrels, these animals remain in one vicinity for their entire lives. This means acceptance of weather conditions and food supplies. Since weather has everything to do with the abundance or scarcity of these animal's vegetable diets, they are factors which most influence their habits. The Lower Sonoran Zone *A. harrisii* inhabits has mild winters which do not force long periods of hibernation on any animal. While cold, windy or wet weather will cause the ground squirrel to retire to its burrow for a few days, it will be out foraging for food on sunny days.

One of the most plentiful foods of late winter and early spring is the fruit of the barrel cactus, *Ferocactus wislizeni*. The large yellow capsules mature in January and February, and are filled with hundreds of small brownish-black seeds. Ground squirrels will eat some on the spot and carry more to their burrows.

The abundance of this food may determine the numbers of young to be produced, because breeding takes place during this period. In late March or early April the five or more young are born.

With the approach of summer, the early annuals have matured and died. The Harris' squirrels eat their fruits and those of the hedgehog and pincushion cactus. July summer rains bring a time of plenty again, and these rodents fatten themselves on the lush vegetation. Late in August the summer rains cease, and the most arid portion of the year comes to the desert. With it arrives the most unusual period of the ground squirrel's life, estivation. In September, although the weather is cooler, the ground temperature can still soar to more than 130°F (54.4°C). The ground squirrels retreat to their cool underground burrows to escape these intolerable conditions. In this sense estivation is like hibernation, except that it is an escape from heat and drought rather than cold. Ground squirrels sleep during hot days, conserving vital moisture in their systems through a slow-down of their body functions, especially the respiratory system.

RANGE: Southern Arizona and northern Sonora, Mexico.

HABITAT: Lower Sonoran Zone. Stony soil on alluvial fans and along rocky washes.

ROUNDTAIL GROUND SQUIRREL

Spermophilus tereticaudus

DESCRIPTION: A small, tan ground squirrel with a sparsely-haired tail. Total length about 9 inches (22.5 centimeters), tail about 3 inches (7.5 centimeters). General body color tan, but lighter underneath, around eyes and legs. The short tail is furry without the flattened effect present in most ground squirrels and chipmunks, hence its specific name *tereticaudus,* meaning round-tailed. Young, four to six, born in early spring with one litter each year.

The roundtail is often associated with the creosotebush in the hot, dry valleys of Arizona and northern Mexico, not so much because it depends on it for food but because the animal and the plant prefer the same soil type. The squirrel's tawny coat blends almost perfectly with the brown clay of the creosote flats.

The roundtail takes advantage of this camouflage when it leaves its burrow. Unlike its relatives, however, it does not climb a vantage point to scout for danger. Instead, it will run a short distance, then settle motionless on the ground surveying the situation with bright, alert eyes. If no danger threatens, it will repeat the performance until it arrives at its destination. If some strange object raises its curiosity, the animal will stand high on its hind legs to see over any low obstacle, using its tail as the third leg of a tripod to keep its balance. With its front paws held against its chest, the roundtail is strongly reminiscent of the "picket pin" of the western prairie. If frightened, it rushes for the closest burrow and may remain underground for the rest of the day.

The life history of the roundtail parallels the Harris' Antelope squirrel's in many ways. They usually emerge from hibernation about the same time. The roundtail, however, depends more on the green food found on the desert floor than *A. harrisii,* which prefers the cactus fruits of the rocky slopes. The roundtail is especially fond of alfilaria *(Erodium* sp.), an introduced plant.

As the season advances, other food becomes available. The short desert grass as well as the leaves of many shrubs are used. These ground squirrels are rather awkward climbers, but they often venture shakily to the end of a limb to reach a particularly tempting bud or tip.

By the middle of March they have regained fat used during hibernation. Great activity is taking place underground, too, remodeling winter nests or preparing new quarters for arrival of the young. The writer was amused at the persistence with which a female tore up a half-page of newspaper lodged in the base of creosotebush near her burrow, carrying it shred by shred to the nest. Usually nests are constructed of grass stems and fibers. Young are born in April and by midsummer are on their own.

The roundtail still observes what is becoming a fast-disappearing custom—the afternoon siesta. By 10 a.m., with a full stomach, it retires from the heat of the surface to the coolness of the burrow. By 3 p.m., as the heat begins dissipating, the roundtail re-emerges from its home until sundown.

This habit is one of necessity, not convenience, for this small rodent. It is part of a survival program that includes eating green food and entering a late summer period of estivation.

This ground squirrel is still relatively abundant within its limited range, but much of its former habitat has been plowed for agriculture.

RANGE: Southern Arizona, California and Nevada and northern Sonora, Mexico.

HABITAT: Lower Sonoran Zone. Desert valleys and low mesas with alluvial soils.

Rock Squirrel

Spermophilus variegatus

DESCRIPTIÓN: Much the same in size and appearance as the eastern gray squirrel. This ground-dwelling rodent is about 20 inches (50 centimeters) long, tail about 9 inches (22.5 centimeters). General color dark gray, front quarters lighter and the hind quarters buffy. Underparts a dirty white, the feet buffy. The bushy gray tail rivals those of the tree squirrels in beauty. Young, from five to ten, born early in the season, from May to July depending on the altitude and latitude.

Variegatus refers to the peculiar coloration of the coat, the front half of the body being a clear gray, while the rear half is sometimes a yellowish brown. With warm weather, the heavy winter hair and undercoat begin to shed from the head and shoulder to be replaced by the thin summer coat. Before this long, slow shedding process is complete the hair of the rear parts has been weathered and sunburned, giving the pelage a definite two-toned cast.

In the rocky terrain that these big ground squirrels frequent, three types of dens are found. In rimrock, many of the nests are built far back in a crevice; in slide rock they are deep among the tumbled mass of talus; on the mesas the squirrel excavates a winding tunnel in the earth between the buried boulders. In most cases the den is safe from all enemies except snakes and ferrets. A vantage point, usually a large rock nearby, provides a place where the squirrel can survey the surrounding terrain. It also serves as a sunbathing spot on cold mornings. Any real or fancied danger is greeted with a loud, shrill whistle that warns any other squirrels in the vicinity. At the first threatening movement the squirrel will slip quietly away to the burrow and remain hidden until it is again safe to venture out.

Rock squirrels are voracious. Their sharp teeth and strong claws can give them entrance to any cabin. No food is safe from them unless encased in tin. These bold animals will climb agave stalks to reach the seed pods, seemingly oblivious to danger from red-tailed hawks. In lower elevations they frequent edges of shallow canyons where the native black walnut grows, gathering numbers of fine-flavored nuts. The husk, when green, is also eaten. Stone fruits and berries are eagerly taken as well as grass seeds, cactus fruits and acorns and pine nuts at higher elevations. Bird eggs and young birds are not often passed by. A thick layer of fat accumulates on the squirrels by fall. In the Transition Zone they disappear for several months during the winter. In the lower desert they retire for only a few weeks. Whether they go into full hibernation during this period is uncertain. Perhaps they enter what might be considered partial hibernation, sleeping for a few days then awakening to eat.

RANGE: Throughout the southwestern states south of the northern borders of Utah and Colorado.

HABITAT: Principally Upper Sonoran Zone, but overlapping into the Lower Sonoran and Transition zones. Rocky terrain with a good cover of trees or shrubs.

SPOTTED GROUND SQUIRREL
Spermophilus spilosoma

DESCRIPTION: A gray-tan ground squirrel with white spots scattered over the back. Total length about 9 inches (22.5 centimeters), tail about 2.75 inches (6.9 centimeters). Color of back gray-brown, dotted noticeably with white spots which may be arranged in lines. The ears are small, the tail sparsely haired. Young, five or more, usually two litters in one season.

While similar in shape and size to the roundtail ground squirrel, part of whose range it shares, the white spots of this group are a certain identifying mark. All of the varieties of this species bear these spots. Appearing rather colorless to those accustomed to the bright spots and stripes of midwestern ground squirrels, it is this drabness that provides protection for this desert-dwelling species. It blends perfectly with the dull soil colors. In addition, this species, like other ground squirrels, has uncanny memory ability. When danger arises, they can find the closest burrow, either their own or one of another rodent.

Its habitat is some of the most barren, inhospitable terrain in the Southwest. Over most of its range, whether stony mesa tops or dry alkali lake beds, vegetation is scant, water is absent and what rain may come in summer downpours quickly runs off the baked surface. Plant life is reduced to species adapted to aridity, soil salinity and animal attack. The most palatable plants have been gleaned by range cattle.

However, cattle have introduced to the open range two plants that provide food for the rodents. One is the native mesquite, which once grew mainly along washes, and another is the Russian thistle. Mesquite beans and foliage provide nourishment, while Russian thistle furnishes seeds and forage when young and succulent.

The spotted ground squirrels gather seeds of all the principal desert grasses and shrubs and eat the young, tender growth of many plants. Cactus flowers and fruits are taken when available, while the pads provide food and moisture during the dry season.

The spotted ground squirrel has a certain advantage by being able to inhabit part of the Upper as well as the Lower Sonoran Zone. The higher elevation means lower temperatures, which makes it unnecessary for it to enter estivation. This summer version of winter hibernation is mandatory for ground squirrels that live in the low, hot valleys. The spotted ground squirrel does, however, hibernate from around the first of December to the first of April.

The spotted ground squirrel produces two litters of young, the first in late spring and second near fall. The old adults are the first to go underground, followed by the young of the spring litter a week or two later. The young of the fall brood are just able to store enough fat to carry them through cold weather.

Geographically *S. spilosoma* links the midwestern striped ground squirrels with the drab, unspotted, unstriped roundtail of the western desert. It has some characteristics common with both.

RANGE: New Mexico, southeastern and northern Arizona, eastern Colorado and west Texas.

HABITAT: Lower and Upper Sonoran zones. Plains and mesas; the burrows are usually located near the bases of low shrubs.

GRAY SHREW
Notiosorex crawfordi

DESCRIPTION: An extremely small, short-tailed animal with prominent ears and tiny eyes. Total length slightly less than 4 inches (10 centimeters), tail a little more than 1 inch (2.5 centimeters) long. General color a dark bluish gray, lighter underneath. Snout long, coming to a point. All the shrews are nervous and irritable in their actions when discovered.

This species, generally considered to be the smallest native mammal, presents a great challenge to scientists. Its rarity, small size and secretive habits make its life history comparatively unknown. What has been discovered, mainly by chance, is extremely interesting. This eared shrew is classed as an insectivore. However, its diet is not exclusively insects and worms. This predator has the innate ferocity of a badger or wolverine, and will not hesitate to do battle with, and sometimes kill small rodents several times its size.

The shrew's story is the story of an appetite mounted on four legs, guided by a keen nose aided by formidable claws and teeth. Throughout the shrew's short life, its unceasing search for food continues, interrupted briefly for sleep and breeding. The shrew would starve to death if it went more than a half day without food. Under these conditions, hibernation is impossible. Presumably it sleeps in a nest taken over from another rodent. The nest in which the young are reared may possibly be built by the mother.

Signs of these shrews might be found in the leaf mold under desert trees and shrubs and in grasslands where tiny tunnels weave through the tangled stems. Any observations of these animals would be welcome information to park naturalists.

RANGE: Most of New Mexico, west Texas, eastern and central Arizona and large parts of Mexico.

HABITAT: The few recorded specimens of this species disclose no definite habitat pattern, but it is believed that they are usually found in loose soils not far from a source of free water.

MEXICAN FREETAIL BAT
Tadarida brasiliensis

DESCRIPTION: A medium-sized dark colored bat with a naked tail extending about 3/4 inch (19.05 millimeters) beyond the tail membrane. The short wide ears are joined over the top of the nose. Wingspread about 10 inches (25 centimeters). The sole young is born in June or July.

Many superstitions and folk tales have grown up concerning the bat family because of their secretive habits and nocturnal life. Bats do not deliberately fly into women's hair. Bats are not airborne rodents; they are flying mammals of the order Chiroptera. Bats are the only mammals that fly in the correct sense of the word. "Flying" squirrels cannot maintain level flight, but glide in a descent from the departure point. No vampire (blood drinking) bats are known in the United States. In this country all are thought to be insect or fruit eaters. The long-nosed bat has a narrow face and specially adapted mouth parts which enable it to gather nectar and this, together with a certain amount of insect prey, forms its food. It is probable some bats may eat other parts of the flowers as well. A fish-catching species of bat is known from the Gulf of California.

On the other hand, many facts about bats remain little known. For instance, bats have the highest rate of heartbeat of any mammal: 700 beats per minute have been recorded. Bats have relatively poor eyesight but remarkably acute hearing. In fact, they fly around objects in total darkness by hearing the echoes of their own voices. Bats' voices are so highly pitched that upper register is inaudible to humans. The lower register in some species can be heard.

Experiments on bats' echolocation systems have uncovered some remarkable information. Bats released in a dark room strung with a few wires emitted a steady succession of squeaks, each about 1/500th second long and 16 per second. No collisions with wires occurred. Tests were continued, with more wires in place. The frequency of the squeaks increased until an average of approximately 60 per second was attained. The bats avoided the wires with few contacts. Then the bats were released with their mouths taped so they could not squeak. They were reluctant to fly, and when they did they blundered into the wires, showing little ability to avoid them. With the tape removed and their ears plugged, results were worse. With only one ear plugged they improved, but flew in circles, veering toward the side with the unplugged ear.

Most bats have extremely large ears that join the face behind the nose. These thin-skinned sonar receivers appear and work much like a parabolic reflector. The slightest sound must be picked up and magnified. Undoubtedly, their ears enable bats to pinpoint the position of flying insects.

Bats have highly specialized bone structure of the front legs, hind legs and tail—all covered with a thin membrane—that has allowed them to master flight. The wings are formed by a shortening of the bones of the front leg, along with a tremendous elongation of the foot bones which support the "fabric." Much like birds fly, the "wings" are partially closed on the upstrokes and extended on the downstroke. Bats are swift fliers. Their seemingly erratic maneuvers are probably skillful darts at insects too small to be seen by human eyes.

The free-tailed bats represent a small part of the species native to North America. In all, over 250 species of bats are listed, many of them in the United States. The total population of bats in the United States is tremendous and may compare to that of the land birds.

Carlsbad Caverns National Park is a famous bat habitat. Although summer populations vary, up to 5 million bats have inhabited the cave in one year. It is estimated that one bat will consume up to its body weight in insects in one night. When the bat population reached 5 million, it is estimated 40 tons (36 metric tons) of insects were consumed in a night.

Before 1923 when the caverns became a national park, bat droppings, or guano, were removed and sold as fertilizer. More than 100,000 tons (90,000 metric tons) of guano were taken and sold for $20 to $75 a ton. Most of the odor around caves and old houses arises from guano deposits. The Mexican freetail bat is one of the worst offenders, but the Mexican people tolerate it because they think the bats control malaria-causing mosquitoes.

Comparatively little is known about the life history of bats. Breeding usually occurs in March, and the young are born in early summer. Many species, including the Mexican freetail, bear one young a year, others up to four. The Mexican freetail does not carry its young in flight, but instead establishes a "nursery" in the cave while the mother spends the night foraging. On her return, she nurses the young. Other bats sometimes carry their young on short flights. The young grow rapidly and can fly 4-6 weeks after birth.

In cold weather bats enter profound hibernation, in which bodily processes slow markedly. The body temperature drops to just above that of the surrounding air. The heartrate slows to a barely perceptible pulse. Hibernation allows the bats to survive during a period when no insect life is available for food.

RANGE: Throughout Mexico and southwest United States.

HABITAT: Caves, crevices in cliffs, mine tunnels, old buildings and under railroad bridges in Upper and Lower Sonoran zones.

WESTERN MASTIFF BAT

Eumops perotis

DESCRIPTION: A large free-tailed bat. Total length about 7 inches (17.5 centimeters), tail projects back of wing about 1 inch (2.5 centimeters). Wingspread 18 to 20 inches (45 to 50 centimeters). General color dark brown. Ears very large, joined over nose. Nostrils especially adapted, giving the face a bulldog appearance. Young, one, born in May or June.

This is the largest bat native to the United States. It is closely related to the Mexican freetail bat, and like that species has a tail that extends free of the wing. Formerly thought to be extremely rare, in recent years it has been found in many localities. In California and Texas it frequents semi-tropical areas where citrus fruit is grown, indicating that it is a fruit-eating bat. Scattered occurrences were also recorded in Arizona, and in the ruins at Casa Grande National Monument a colony was discovered, the only large one known in the state. Although living on the edge of an agricultural area, the Casa Grande group is some distance from any large fruit-growing area, thus the bats are presumably eating insects.

The distribution of this species is irregular. It is plentiful in some sections west of the coastal range in southern California, rare in Arizona, unrecorded in New Mexico, and of limited occurrence in southern Texas. About 20 form an average size colony, and a maximum of 70 in one group has been recorded. Many solitary specimens have been found.

Little is known of the life history of these big bats. The breeding season is late fall and early winter. The development of the embryo slows while the female is hibernating, and the young are not born until the following May or June. Adults commonly roost alone in a crevice or close together on some horizontal support. They can flatten their bodies so that a very narrow crack will accommodate them. With the sharp claws of the hind feet and the single claw on the wings they easily cling to any roughened surface. Unlike most other species of bats, they do not shun the light. They will accept almost any roost as long as it is not exposed to the sun's direct heat. Most individuals prefer to roost at least 30 feet (9 meters) above the ground because when they take flight they release their hold with the hind feet before they open their wings.

One of this bat's most remarkable features is its large ears. At rest, the ears droop over the small eyes and join over the nose to produce an unusual effect. When in use, the ears curve like two shells and are highly efficient at picking up sounds. At their highest extension the convex surfaces almost touch above the head.

RANGE: In the Southwest; southern Texas, southern Arizona and southern California.

HABITAT: Lower Sonoran Zone. High cliff walls, old houses and trees.

BLACKTAIL PRAIRIE DOG
Cynomys ludovicianus

DESCRIPTION: A large, heavily-built ground squirrel with short legs and tail. Total length about 15 inches (37.5 centimeters), tail about 3.5 inches (8.75 centimeters). Color a sandy tan, somewhat lighter underneath and around the eyes; tail with black tip. Ears short. Face resembles that of a woodchuck. Front feet armed with long stout claws; those of hind feet shorter. The four or five young are born early in May and by midsummer are able to gather their own food.

One of the most vociferous southwestern mammals, its rapid series of "yaps" has earned it the name "dog." Trills, whistles and chatters, more ground squirrel-like, are frequently used. The clamor of a prairie dog town can be heard for some distance—the volume swelling and fading. This general hubbub of "conversation" and the prairie dogs' eternal watchfulness make excellent defense against approaching predators. Once the stalker is spotted, the prairie dogs retreat to their underground burrows, with periodic peeks from the mounds to determine whether the danger is past. Predators, including eagles, hawks, foxes and bobcats, sometimes outwit them. Their burrows are not snake-proof and badgers can dig them out. Coyotes have broken the system by traveling in pairs. One stays by the mound while the other walks away. As the prairie dogs emerge from their burrows and see that the threat has apparently past, the coyote that stayed near the mound makes the kill.

The prairie dog's burrow is under a cone-shaped mound of excavated earth. Its slope helps shed rain and its elevation provides a point from which to survey the surroundings. The main shaft of the burrow extends nearly vertically into the ground for 10 to 20 feet (3 to 6 meters), leveling out into a long horizontal tunnel with several short side tunnels branching off. This deep burrow insulates the prairie dog from heat or cold. Its purpose is not to reach water, as is sometimes believed. A small emergency tunnel is dug off the main shaft just below the surface in case of flooding.

The ground around the burrow is completely bare, giving no cover to other living things. Surrounding this bare spot is an area of grass and weeds for food. In lean years, the rodents may be forced to go farther afield in search of any cactus, bark or twigs that can sustain them.

Prairie dogs learn the routine of colony life at a young age. At a signal from mother of any nearby danger, they dive simultaneously into the burrow. In late summer they begin to store fat to survive winter's hibernation. They do not retire for their winter "sleep" as early in the year as the elders do since they have not had as much time to fatten.

RANGE: West Texas, New Mexico and eastern Colorado.

HABITAT: Mainly Upper Sonoran Zone. Grasslands on prairies and mesas.

REFERENCES

Burt, William Henry, and Grossenheider, Richard Phillip. 1952. *The Field Guide to the Mammals.* Boston: Houghton Mifflin Co., The Riverside Press, Cambridge.

Cockrum, E. Lendell.

1960. *The Recent Mammals of Arizona: Their Taxonomy and Distribution.* Tucson: University of Arizona Press.

1982. *Mammals of the Southwest.* Tucson: University of Arizona Press.

Dobie, J. Frank. 1949. *The Voice of the Coyote.* Boston: Little, Brown.

Jaeger, Edmund C. 1957. *The North American Deserts.* Stanford: Stanford University Press.

Kirk, Ruth, and Kirk, Lewis. 1973. *Desert: The American Southwest.* Boston: Houghton Mifflin Co.

Larson, Peggy, and Larson, Lane. 1977. *Sierra Club Naturalist's Guide to the Deserts of the Southwest.* San Francisco: Sierra Club Press.

Miller and Kellogg. 1955. *List of North American Recent Mammals.* United States National Museum Bulletin #205. Washington, D.C.: Government Printing Office.

National Geographic Society. 1979. *Wild Animals of North America.* Washington, D.C.: National Geographic.

Zim, Herbert S., and Hoffmeister, Donald F. 1955. *Mammals, A Golden Nature Guide.* New York: Simon and Schuster.